WHITTLING

"Whittlin' Bill" Higginbotham at work.

WHITTLING

Bill Higginbotham

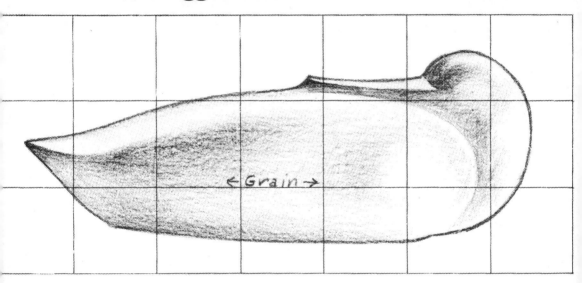

←Grain→

STERLING PUBLISHING COMPANY, INC.   New York
Distributed in the U.K. by Blandford Press

To my dear wife, Frances, whose persistent encouragement motivated me to produce this book.

Edited and designed by Hannah Reich

Library of Congress Cataloging in Publication Data
Higginbotham, Bill.
    Whittling.

    (Home craftsman series)
    Includes index.
    1. Wood-carving. I. Title. II. Series.
TT199.7.H533   736'.4   81-85041
ISBN 0-8069-7598-9 (pbk.)   AACR2

Fifth Printing, 1984

Copyright © 1983 by Sterling Publishing Co., Inc.
Two Park Avenue, New York, N.Y. 10016
Distributed in Australia by Oak Tree Press Co., Ltd.
P.O. Box K514 Haymarket, Sydney 2000, N.S.W.
Distributed in the United Kingdom by Blandford Press
Link House, West Street, Poole, Dorset BH15 1LL, England
Distributed in Canada by Oak Tree Press Ltd.
℅ Canadian Manda Group, P.O. Box 920, Station U
Toronto, Ontario, Canada M8Z 5P9
Manufactured in the United States of America

TABLE OF CONTENTS

ACKNOWLEDGMENTS

My appreciation and thanks to the following people for their assistance in the preparation of this book: Chuck Bayless, who furnished the excellent carvings used on pages 34, 45, 49, and 53 to 76; Helen Caraveo, who drew all the fine patterns; Randy Dunn, who produced all the photographs except those credited to Gary Covington; Gary Covington, who greatly assisted with the photography; Van Smith, who provided all the knives except the two on the far right in Figure 1; Erwin Caldwell, who whittled the Minidove; and W. R. Case and Sons, who presented me with one of their quality pocketknives.

I would also like to thank my many woodcarving friends for their many excellent ideas and suggestions.

PREFACE

This book is designed to help beginners learn the fascinating art of creating projects from wood. A knife is the principal tool needed for all the projects except one, the tiki. Carving wood with a knife is called whittling. Most of the projects in this book were whittled.

The projects are organized according to difficulty. The student will gradually proceed from very simple figures to more complex projects.

This book is also designed to aid arts and crafts and industrial arts instructors teach the challenging art of carving in wood. Teachers of these subjects are often confronted with students who are difficult to motivate. These students need something to challenge their imaginations. Whittling provides that challenge.

Leaders of Boy Scout and Cub Scout troops will find this how-to book an aid to scouts in their pursuit of merit badges on woodcarving. It will also help parents answer the oft-asked question, "What can I do now?"

For twenty-four years I taught crafts in the public and state schools of California and Utah. Wood whittling was my core craft. The students would commence whittling the first day they entered my classes. After they had mastered the techniques, they would proceed to learn other crafts. The experience and skills derived from whittling would carry over to the other crafts (leathercraft, ceramics, mosaics, and plastic crafts.) If interest lagged in one of these, the student would invariably return to whittling, which was inexpensive, challenging, and satisfying.

I suggest that the beginner start with the first project and complete each in sequence until he or she feels enough self-confidence to skip to more advanced projects.

The stylized types are placed in the early part of the book because of their simplicity and ease in carving. They help the carver to learn the art of proportioning, which is so necessary for any type of successful carving.

As you progress through this book I hope you experience the satisfaction and joy that results from creating useful and attractive figures in wood.

Happy Whittling!
Bill Higginbotham
St. George, Utah

Figure 1. A collection of eight hand-made whittling knives. The factory-made knife is the second from the right.

Figure 2. Honing the blade on an oilstone. (Photo by G. Covington.)

8

CARVING TOOLS

These tools consist of knives, chisels, gouges, rasps, and sanding sticks. The particular tools employed in this book are knives, chisels, rasps, and sanding sticks. Some carvers prefer hand-held power carving tools, like flexible-shaft machines equipped with grinding or cutting bits. All tools designed to remove unwanted wood are classified as carving tools.

The stylized figures in this book may be carved by using a combination of knives, rasps, and sanding sticks. The very simple shapes such as the mouse may be shaped with sanding sticks. Smaller children quickly adapt themselves to the use of this tool.

However, many carvers, myself included, favor the knife as the primary carving tool. The feel of a sharp blade cutting away wood is an enjoyable experience.

When I first started teaching high school arts and crafts in 1956, the first subject introduced was whittling. The lack of knives was temporarily solved by a visit to the local police station. In response to my request for knives, the lieutenant in charge presented me with a collection of confiscated switchblade knives. These served as poor substitutes for carving tools until a supply of German-made whittling knives were obtained. These knives may be purchased from craft and woodcarving supply stores. (See Figure 1, second knife from the far right.)

Factory-made whittling knives are unsharpened when they leave the factory. It requires an hour or more of honing on an oilstone or a whetstone to produce a wire edge. Most writers of woodcarving books recommend that the back edge of the blade be elevated slightly when honing. I prefer to press the blade flat against the stone, as illustrated in Figure 2. This produces a wide bevel on the blade edge. For soft or semi-hardwood the wide bevel works best. A narrow bevel edge is best for hardwoods. When cutting hardwood, the wide bevel edge tends to develop nicks.

Apply a small amount of thin oil to an oilstone, or water to a whetstone, before running the blade back and forth on the stone. The water or oil floats away the metal particles that are ground from the knife blade. You will observe in Figure 2 that the forefinger of the left hand exerts pressure against the blade as it travels in the direction of the arrow. Before the blade reaches the end of the stone, the finger pressure is removed. The knife blade is turned over and, again pressing the forefinger on the blade, it is drawn sharp-edge first toward the person sharpening it. This back-and-forth movement is repeated until a wire edge develops.

Remove the wire edge by stropping the blade on an abrasive strop. (See Figure 3.) This strop is made by gluing or stapling a piece of sponge rubber, suede, or felt onto a ¾-inch (1.9-cm)-thick piece of 1½-inch (3.8-cm)-wide piece of wood. Over this cushiony material is tacked or stapled a strip of emery cloth or wet or dry sandpaper. (See Figure 4.) Number 240 grit emery cloth or fine (#180 grit) wet or dry sandpaper is recommended. Emery cloth and sandpaper may be purchased from automotive supply shops or from hardware store dealers.

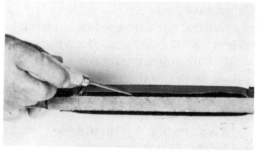

Figure 4. Sponge-rubber backing between the emery cloth and the wood. This strop has #240 grit on one side and #300 on the other.

Figure 3. Stropping the blade on an emery strop.

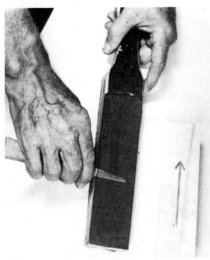

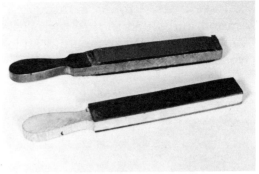

Figure 6. Useful emery and leather strops. Overall length of these strops is 13¾ inches (34.9 cm).

Figure 5. Final stropping on leather dressed with petroleum jelly and fine carborundum dust. This dust may be purchased at lapidary stores.

A further refining of the edge may be accomplished by stropping back and forth on a leather strop. Glue a strip of leather or suede onto the side of the wood opposite the emery cloth. (See Figures 5 and 6.)

A quality pocketknife, as shown in Figure 7, is a very good whittling knife. Many whittlers prefer the pocketknife above all other knives. Since it can be carried in the pocket, it is available for use whenever the opportunity arises. When selecting the knife, make certain the blades are not stainless steel. Stainless steel is very difficult to sharpen and is unsuitable for carving wood. New pocketknife blades are not honed sharp. It is necessary to hone and strop them in order to ready them for whittling. Use the same sharpening techniques as described above.

Wood rasps, as illustrated in Figure 8, are very useful for removing excess wood. Stylized carvings are easily rasped to shape. The rasp is recommended for beginners and especially for younger children. It is a safe tool. Also shown in Figure 8 are several half-round sanding sticks. A sanding stick is easy to make. Merely glue a strip of sandpaper to a stick. Tongue depressors make good sanding sticks. For sanding in concave areas, a round sanding stick is useful. Sandpaper wrapped around and glued to a ½-inch (1.3-cm) or ¾-inch (1.9-cm) dowel is simple to make. Younger children feel very comfortable sanding away wood with these simple abrasive tools.

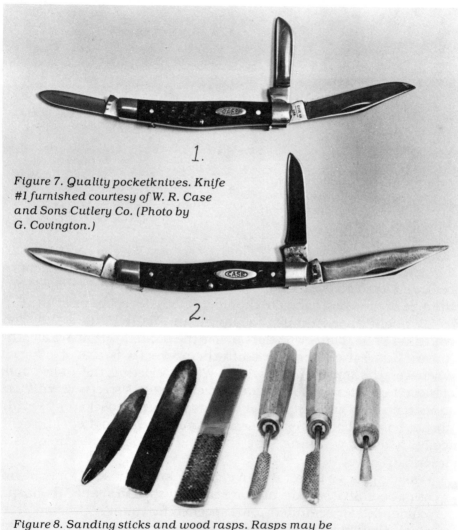

Figure 7. Quality pocketknives. Knife #1 furnished courtesy of W. R. Case and Sons Cutlery Co. (Photo by G. Covington.)

Figure 8. Sanding sticks and wood rasps. Rasps may be purchased from craft stores and woodcarving supply shops.

PATTERNS AND THEIR USE

The patterns in this book are shaded to assist you in visualizing the shape and proportion of the finished carvings. The patterns were sketched from the completed carvings.

If you wish to make patterns from ceramic, plaster, or wooden figurines, use the shadow method as demonstrated in Figures 9 and 10. The model is placed in front of a piece of translucent plastic or frosted glass. If you wish to use plastic, lightly sand a transparent piece of plastic to achieve the translucence. A piece of tracing paper is taped onto the opposite side of the plastic or glass. In a darkened room a high intensity beam of light is focussed on the model. The shadow patterns are traced as shown in Figure 10. The resultant pattern will be slightly larger than the original model.

The pantograph shown in Figure 11 is used to decrease or increase the size of the pattern. This machine will make an exact reproduction in either a larger or smaller size. It may be purchased in arts and crafts supply shops or from wood carving suppliers.

Ideas for patterns may also be found in newspapers, magazines, or books. Some may be hidden in your mind, waiting to be developed. Patterns are invaluable to the whittler because they serve as guides in the process of cutting out figures to prescribed designs. If a person had to carve from an uncut block of wood, it would be very difficult and time-consuming. Cutting and whittling from a pattern simplifies the carving process.

FINISHING

The finishing process should require almost as much time as the initial carving of the project. For a stylized figure, considerable sanding is necessary to prepare the wood for the final finish. Unless a person is quite adept at shaving wood smoothly with a knife, the whittled project should also receive a thorough sanding.

Figure 9. The model placed between the high intensity light and the translucent plastic.

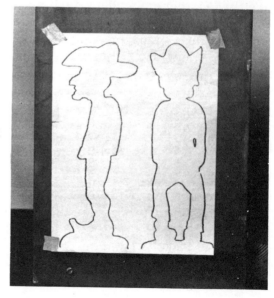

Figure 10. Profile and rear-view patterns traced from Cowpoke Charley's shadows.

Figure 11. Use of the pantograph to enlarge a pattern.

The final finishing of stylized and realistic or caricature-like projects differ. The instructions for finishing stylized figures are given first.

FINISHING A STYLIZED FIGURE

Step 1. After the carving has been roughed out and shaped to the final form with a knife or rasp, sand it with coarse sandpaper across the grain of the wood.

Step 2. Use medium grit sandpaper (#120) to remove all major rasp, knife, and coarse-sandpaper marks. Sand with the grain of the wood.

Step 3. Rub the surface with a very fine sandpaper to produce a satin-smooth finish.

Step 4. Douse the figure with water. *Do not* soak the wood. The application of water will raise the wood fibres.

Step 5. When the carving is thoroughly dry, resand with extra fine sandpaper. (The wetting, drying, and fine-sanding should be repeated several times until the wood feels super slick.) After sanding, dust the wood, to remove any fine particles of wood.

Step 6. Spray or brush a coat of clear lacquer, varnish, or shellac onto the wood surface.

Step 7. Allow sufficient time for thorough drying, then sand with extra-fine sandpaper. Apply a second coat of varnish or lacquer.

Step 8. Rub the dried surface with fine steel wool impregnated with a good grade of clear paste wax. Follow the polishing directions given on the can.

ALTERNATE METHOD

If desired, the lacquer or varnish may be eliminated and the wax applied directly to the bare wood. Several coats of clear paste wax will improve the appearance. Polish with a clean soft cloth in between applications of wax and after the final coat.

FINISHING REALISTIC OR CARICATURE CARVINGS

Step 1. Remove dirt and smudge marks with a knife or with sandpaper. If the figure is not carved smoothly, follow the sanding procedure described previously for stylized figures.

Step 2. Paint the finished carving with water-based paints, such as poster paints, water colors, or acrylics. They are easy to apply and the brushes may be cleaned with water. However, if you prefer to use oil colors or stains, thin them with turpentine or Danish Oil. I prefer Danish Oil as a vehicle. It dries in a reasonable time to a durable finish.

Step 3. After the paint or stain is thoroughly dry, a light sanding with fine sandpaper helps accentuate the highlights and the knife cuts. To avoid smearing, use small squares of sandpaper and rub the individual colors lightly.

CARVING WOODS

It is important to exercise care in the selection of wood for carving and whittling. What may be desirable for rasping figures to shape may not be suitable for whittling. However, most of the woods described below may be used for either rasping or whittling. Preferred carving woods should be free from sap, pitch, or resin. These substances adhere to the teeth of the rasp and soon render it ineffective unless cleaned often with a wire brush. Sappy or resinous materials in the wood also bleed through the finish.

Use wood with a distinct grain for stylized figures. It results in the most attractive finished effect. Whittling wood should be soft or semi-hard, but not spongy like balsa. However, it is possible to purchase dense balsa that is suitable for whittling. A good whittling wood allows the carver to cut across the grain without tearing. It should be of even, firm texture and free from excessive grain.

This chapter is divided into two sections. The first section describes woods that are especially good for rasping. The second section lists woods most suitable for carving with a knife.

WOODS FOR RASPING

Redwood: This wood does not load the rasp and carves easily with a rasp. Even the grainy pieces are easy to shape and finish up beautifully. Soft, clear redwood makes good whittling wood.

Juniper (red cedar): This is another wood that responds well to rasping. It does not load the rasp. The *common juniper* is found throughout the northern hemisphere. It does not grow in tropical regions. In Utah it is used for fence posts and firewood. The yellow and white streaks that mingle with the red produce an attractive effect when finished. Straight-grained red or yellow cedar is also a pleasure to whittle.

Exotic Hardwoods: Cocobolo, teak, and zebrawood may be rasped into attractive projects. I have carved many whittling knife handles from these woods with a rasp. The superb finish that one achieves after much sanding and rubbing is well worth the time spent working with these beautiful woods. However, the cost of exotic hardwoods is almost prohibitive. They are usually sold by the pound, unlike more common woods, which are sold by the board foot.

Walnut: Popular among many wood-carvers who carve with chisels and gouges, it responds well to rasping, being devoid of loading substances. Walnut is expensive, but the finished product is well worth the cost.

Oak: If you like to work with hardwoods, oak, despite its graininess, is not too difficult to shape with a rasp. The finished product is well worth the extra effort required to shape this rather tough wood.

WOODS FOR WHITTLING

Basswood (linden): This is placed first among the woods most preferred for whittling. The lack of grain in this wood makes it possible to cut it in most any direction without tearing, chipping, or splitting. It is excellent for carving in fine detail in faces or hands. The famous carvers of Germany and Switzerland, as well as many excellent whittlers and wood-carvers of North America, prefer basswood.

White Pine: An excellent wood for whittling because of its very close, even grain. It is almost devoid of grain, which makes it very suitable for fine-detail carving.

Sugar Pine: Another close-grained wood. The sugar spots in the wood give it a pleasing appearance. Some sugar pine is quite hard and grainy, so the whittler must select with care.

Aspen: This wood is plentiful in the higher elevations of the western part of the United States. An air-dried, well seasoned piece of aspen is similar to basswood in texture. I always keep a plentiful supply of aspen logs on hand for carving. The colors of the heartwood vary from white to light tan. Dead, standing trees, if not beetle-infected, insure well seasoned whittling wood.

Miscellaneous Whittling Woods: Cottonwood, willow, and poplar are used by whittlers. These woods also respond to rasping because they are free from loading resins.

If you live in an area where any of the above woods grow, secure a permit from the United States Forest Service and cut your own carving wood. Seal the ends of the logs with shellac, lacquer, or sealing wax. Leave the bark on the logs, and place them in a shady place with plenty of ventilation so the air may reach all parts of the logs. They will then dry uniformly, minimizing the risk of splitting and checking. Drying time is usually about a year.

I prefer dry, well seasoned wood for whittling. Some carvers like to whittle green wood. It is easier to cut, especially if you cut the tree in the winter when the sap has gone down to the roots. If you wish to prevent the wood from drying out when you are not working on it, keep it submerged in water. However, do not leave green wood in water for long periods of time. Continuous soaking darkens the color of the wood.

Strange as it may seem, green wood ordinarily does not check or split after it has been carved. The fact that the air can reach all areas of the wood prevents this from happening, because it dries uniformly.

Figure 12. The goose and the gander, whittled from basswood.

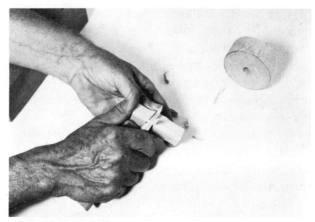

Figure 13. The thumb-pull method. The knife is under control and removes shavings, not chunks of wood.

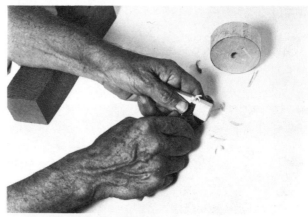

Figure 14. Here the knife is held firmly in the right hand, while the left thumb pushes it. This is a precise and safe method of whittling.

Figure 15. The wood block is braced against a piece of wood that is clamped to the bench. This is another very safe way to carve.

WHITTLING TECHNIQUES

Whittling is the art of carving wood with a knife. It is a convenient method of sculpting. Knife carving eliminates the need for a workbench, vise, and other equipment required for carving with chisels and gouges. Since the carving piece is held in the hand—a superior vise—it can be turned in any direction with ease.

When I attended football, basketball, and baseball games, my pocketknife and wood cutout always accompanied me. I could whittle during huddles, warm-ups, and between halves and innings.

A large number of people have the ability to whittle but do not realize it. One of the purposes of this book is to help those individuals discover their potential. A good preliminary project is the dowel. It will serve to introduce you to the fascinating process of removing wood with a sharp knife. Select a ¾ x ¾ x 2-inch (1.9 x 1.9 x 5.08-cm)-piece of soft, straight-grained wood. Your goal is to gradually whittle this piece down to a ⅜-inch (9.5-mm) dowel. Study Figures 13–15 to learn the basic whittling cuts. Continue to turn the wood in your fingers as you whittle away the excess stock. Remove thin shavings rather than large chunks.

A well-carved dowel should be symmetrical along its length. It should barely pass through a ⅜-inch (9.5-mm) hole. (See Figure 16.) If you do not succeed in carving a smooth, even dowel, try again until you are successful.

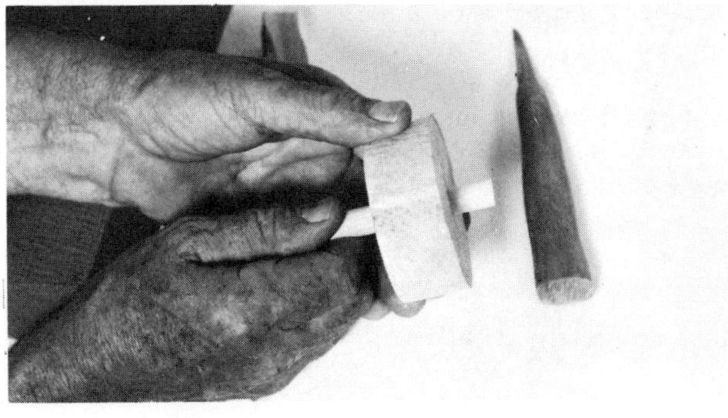

Figure 16. The dowel is carved so precisely that it will barely pass through the ⅜-inch (9.5-mm) hole.

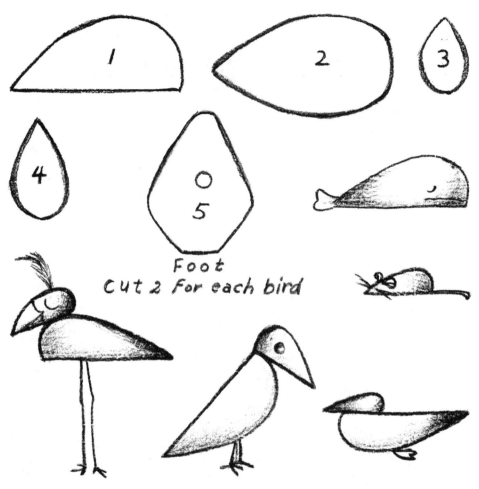

Figure 17. Patterns for mice, rats, and birds.

Figure 18. Side-view pattern of the mouse, traced onto a block of wood. The figure on the right is the mouse blocked out and ready for shaping.

MICE AND A RAT

The simplicity and universal appeal of a carved mouse makes it a good beginning project. It may be shaped with a sharp knife, small wood rasp, or a coarse sanding stick. It is recommended that younger children use a rasp or a sanding stick to shape the mouse. These tools are safer and easier to manipulate.

Redwood is suggested because it rasps easily. It also carves easily with a knife, provided the wood is not too grainy. Also, the color of the wood is attractive when varnished or waxed. However, some carvers prefer pine or other white softwood for the mouse.

A well-shaped mouse may be formed by following the step-by-step instructions outlined below.

PROCEDURES FOR CARVING

Step 1. Trace a side view from the pattern sheet. (See Figure 17, item 1.) Transfer this pattern to a piece of carving wood that is 1 inch thick x 1 inch wide x 2 inches long (2.5 cm x 2.5 cm x 5 cm). (See Figure 18.)

Step 2. Saw out the silhouette with either a coping, band, or jig saw. Figure 18 also shows the mouse blocked out ready for rounding to shape.

Step 3. Round off the corners with a knife, rasp, or sanding stick. (See Figure 19.)

Figure 19. Rounding the body with a sanding stick.

Figure 20. Punching the ear hole with an awl.

Figure 21. Drilling the ear hole with a ⅛-inch (3.2-mm)-diameter drill.

Figure 22. Using a sharp awl to punch in whisker holes.

Step 4. Rough-sand the half-round figure until it is fairly smooth.

Step 5. Use an awl to punch the holes for the ears as shown in Figure 20.

Step 6. Drill shallow ⅛-inch (3.2-mm) diameter holes for the ears. (Refer to Figure 21.)

Step 7. Use a large needle or a sharp awl to punch in five small holes on either side of the nose. These holes are for the whiskers which will be inserted later. (See Figure 22.)

Step 8. If necessary, finish rounding the mouse with a fine sanding stick. (See Figure 23.) Sand the carving satin smooth.

Step 9. Apply clear paste wax to the wood. Polish to a high lustre with a soft cloth.

Step 10. Use scissors to cut two teardrop-shaped ears from suede, thin leather, or felt. The ear pattern is shown in Figure 17, item 3. Dip the pointed ends of the ears in wood glue before inserting them into the ear holes.

Step 11. Bristles pulled from a counter brush or paint brush serve as whiskers. Dip an end of the bristle in white glue. Then insert it into the whisker hole on either side of the nose. Repeat this until all ten holes are filled with bristles.

Step 12. Small round dressmaker pins serve for eyes. Use wire cutters to shorten the shank of the pin to ¼ inch (6.4 mm). Punch eye holes with an awl so the eyes will be recessed into the wood. Rhinestones may be used for eyes. Glue them on with wood glue or with Epoxy Super Glue.

Step 13. For the tail use a short (2–3-inch) (5–7.6-cm) length of leather lacing or a narrow slice of leather, suede, or felt. Drill a 1/16 inch (1.6 mm) diameter hole about ¼ inch (6.4 mm) deep into the rear end of the mouse body. Dip an end of the tail into white glue and insert that end into drilled hole.

Figure 23. Smoothing the body with an extra-fine sanding stick.

25

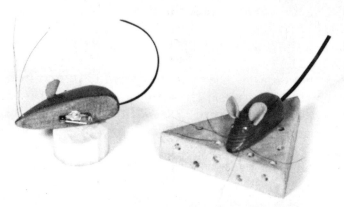

Figure 24. Mouse with pin back and mouse mounted on a simulated wedge of cheese.

If you wish, a pin back may be secured to the bottom of the mouse with a tiny screw, a brad with a head, or Epoxy Super Glue (see Figure 24). Pin backs may be purchased at hobby or craft stores. My son developed a thriving business selling this kind of mouse to girls in his high school to be worn on their blouses or sweaters.

The mouse may be mounted on a simulated wedge of cheese as illustrated in Figure 24. Drill a number of 3/16-inch (4.8-mm)-diameter holes into a pie-shaped wedge of wood. Paint it a yellowish orange before glueing the mouse onto it.

Figure 25. The production of the mouse in a five stage sequence. Note the little spot of black paint for the nose on the finished mouse.

Figure 26. The finished rat.

A rat (see Figure 26) may also be made by following the same procedure given for the mouse. Refer to Figure 28a, item 4 for the rat pattern. Item 4 on Figure 17 is a pattern for the ear. Cut a longer tail and whiskers. Rhinestones, movable eyes, or larger dressmaker pins may be used for eyes. These items may be purchased from hobby or craft stores. The eyes of the rat shown in Figure 26 are 3/16-inch (4.8-mm)-diameter pearl beads. They are partially recessed into the wood. The pupils are painted-on spots of black lacquer.

Perhaps you would like to produce a family of mice as shown in Figure 27. This group, consisting of a father, mother, and several baby mice, is a fun project.

Figure 27. The mouse family.

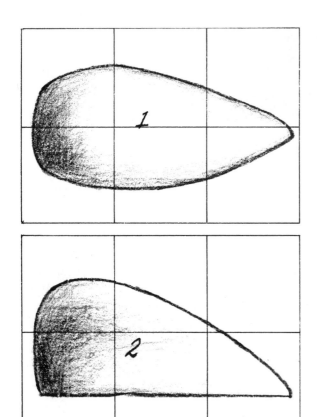

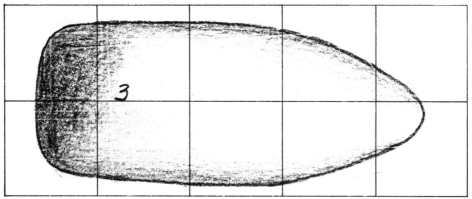

Figure 28. Patterns for birds and rats.

1 sq. = 1 inch (2.54 cm)

BIRDS AND MORE BIRDS

Birds are made by using patterns similar to those used for mice and the rat. The techniques learned while shaping mice will aid you in making birds. These birds are easy to carve with either a rasp, knife, or sanding stick. The birds displayed in the following photographs were made with wood rasps. Redwood was used because it's easy to rasp and has a nice grain.

PROCEDURES FOR CARVING

Step 1. Trace the head and body patterns from pattern sheets.

Step 2. Transfer the body patterns to a 2-inch x 2-inch x 4-inch (5-cm x 5-cm x 10-cm)-long piece of redwood, cedar, or any wood with a distinctive grain.

Step 3. Saw the top view almost through, as shown in Figure 29. Next, saw out the profile view. (See Figure 30.) Figure 31 shows a blocked-out body ready for rounding with knife, rasp, or coarse sanding stick.

Step 4. Follow the same procedure described in Step 3 to block out the head.

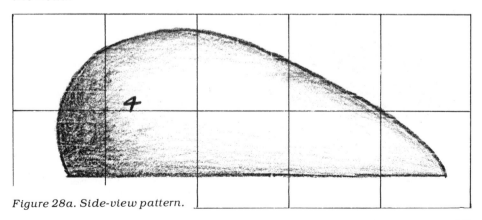

Figure 28a. Side-view pattern.

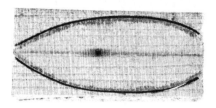

Figure 29. Top view of bird body almost sawed through.

Figure 30. Profile view of the body sawed out.

Step 5. Round off all the corners so the finished product resembles the models shown in Figure 32.

Step 6. Trace and transfer the foot pattern (Figure 17, item 5) to two ¼-inch (6.4-mm)-thick pieces of wood.

Step 7. Drill 3/16-inch (4.8-mm)-holes in the feet as shown in Figure 17, item 9.

Step 8. Saw out the feet. Round off the corners of the feet with a medium-grit sanding stick. Leave the bottom of the feet flat.

Step 9. Drill 3/16-inch (4.8-mm)-diameter neck holes in the top-part of the body and the underside of the head. Drill to a depth of about ¾ inch (1.9 cm).

Figure 31. Bird body blocked out.

Figure 32. Head and body shaped and sanded smooth.

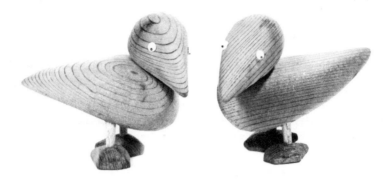

Figure 33. Birds finished but unvarnished.

Step 10. Use an awl to mark the location of the leg holes in the body. In order to be on target, drill ⅛-inch (3.2-mm)-diameter-pilot holes through the awl marks. Drill through the pilot holes with a ¼-inch (6.4-mm) bit to a ⅜-inch (9.6-mm) depth. For aid in locating the leg holes refer to Figures 33 and 34.

Step 11. Cut a short length off a 3/16-inch (4.8-mm) dowel rod for the neck. Also cut 2 pieces of ¼-inch (6.4-mm) dowel 1½-inches (3.8-cm) long for the legs of the birds shown in Figure 33. The legs of the birds in Figure 34 may vary in length, so cut to fit.

Step 12. Use a knife, rasp, or sanding stick to taper the legs from ¼-inch (6.4-mm) diameter to 3/16-inch (4.8-mm) diameter to fit into the holes in the feet.

Figure 34. Long-legged birds.

FINISHING

Step 1. Sand the body, head, legs, and feet until satin smooth. Dust clean.

Step 2. Cement movable eyes to the head with Super Glue or wood glue. (See Figures 33 and 34 for help in locating the eye position.)

Step 3. Spray or brush several coats of clear lacquer or varnish onto the head, body, legs, and feet. Sand in between coats with very fine sandpaper, then dust. Exercise special care when sanding around the movable eyes.

Step 4. Rub all the above parts with fine steel wool impregnated with clear paste wax. Polish with a soft cloth to a high lustre.

Step 5. Fasten the head to the body with the previously cut 3/16-inch (4.8-mm) dowel. Glue the dowel into the body hole, but leave the head loose so it can be turned as desired.

Step 6. Glue the legs into the body and leg holes.

The stylized whale and dove shown in Figures 35 and 36 were made by modifying the bird-body pattern (Figure 28a, item 4). The narrow end of the body was extended to create the whale's tail. The dove was created by rounding off the flukes of the whale's tail.

Figure 35. Whale made from bird pattern.

Figure 36. Dove made by rounding off the whale's tail flukes.

PENNY, THE WREN

This small stylized bird is rather easy to whittle or rasp to shape. The wren shown in Figure 43 was whittled from a piece of sycamore wood. This medium hard, reddish-brown wood is close-grained. It has a beautiful grain and finishes well.

Penny is a good project to carve with a knife. She fits well into the holding hand. If she is cut out two ways, top and profile view, it is simple to round her to shape with a sharp whittling knife.

PROCEDURES FOR CARVING

Step 1. Trace and transfer the top view pattern, Figure 37, to a piece of carving wood that measures 2 inches x 2 inches x 5 inches (5 cm x 5 cm x 12.70 cm) long. Next, trace and transfer the profile view, Figure 38, to the side of this oblong block of wood.

Step 2. Commence by sawing the top view first. Stop sawing about 1/16 of an inch (1.6 mm) from the rear end of the pattern. (See Figure 39.)

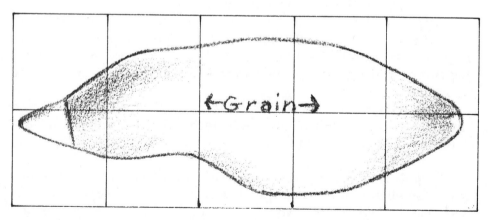

Figure 37. Top-view pattern of Penny, the Wren.   *1 sq. = 1 inch (2.54 cm)*

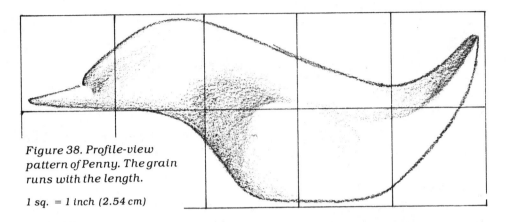

Figure 38. Profile-view pattern of Penny. The grain runs with the length.

1 sq. = 1 inch (2.54 cm)

Step 3. Saw out the profile view. (See Figure 40.) Pull the sawed pieces apart and you will have a blocked-out figure ready for shaping. (See Figure 41.)

Step 4. Use a knife, rasp, or a coarse sanding stick to round off the sharp corners. A well-shaped wren should feel smooth and symmetrical. (See Figure 42.) Be very careful when carving around the beak. Use a small fine sanding stick to complete this delicate part.

FINISHING

Step 1. Sand the wren until it is very smooth.

Step 2. Moisten the surface of the wood with a damp sponge to raise the grain. Allow sufficient time for thorough drying and then resand with extra-fine sandpaper until the bird feels satin smooth. Repeat the wetting, drying, and sanding process. Wipe away any wood dust.

Step 3. Spray the entire bird with clear plastic, lacquer, or varnish. Let it dry overnight. Sand the surface with extra-fine or worn-out sandpaper. Apply a second coat of clear sealer. Again allow it to dry overnight.

Step 4. Rub the sealed surface with fine steel wool impregnated with a small amount of clear paste wax. Polish to a deep, rich shine with a soft, clean cloth. If you desire a higher lustre, apply a second coat of wax, and polish.

34

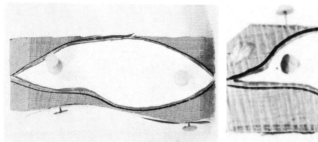

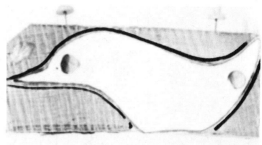

Figure 39. The top view is sawed to within ¹/₁₆ of an inch (1.6 mm) from the rear end of the pattern. Note: The pattern is thumbtacked to the wood.

Figure 40. Side-view band sawed out to pattern shape.

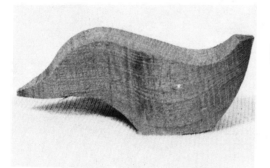

Figure 41. Penny blocked out, ready for rounding to shape.

Figure 42. Penny whittled to shape, ready for finishing.

Figure 43. Wren whittled out of sycamore wood by C. Bayless.

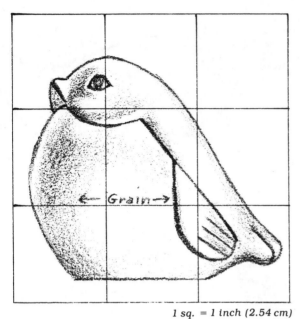

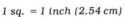

Figure 44. The profile-view pattern of the Minidove.

1 sq. = 1 inch (2.54 cm)

1 sq. = 1 inch (2.54 cm)

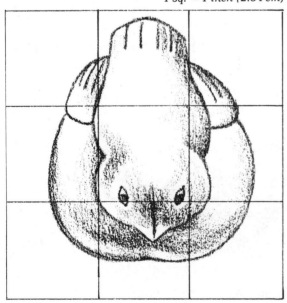

Figure 45. Top view of the Minidove.

A MINIDOVE

This small dove is not too difficult to carve, provided it is cut out two ways on the band saw. Refer to Penny, the Wren (pp. 33–35) for a description of the compound cutting method used to block out the wren.

Use a sharp whittling knife to round off the edges of the wood cutout. Outline the wings by making a vertical cut along the wing pattern lines. Then cut on an angle to meet the vertical incision. If this is done with care and skill, you should be able to remove a narrow sliver all along the wing line.

Use a small-bladed knife to detail the head section, eyes, and beak. Refer frequently to the patterns (Figures 44 and 45) and to the photo (Figure 46) for aid. Use extra care when carving the beak and eyes.

FINISHING

Sand the entire figure until satin smooth. Follow the same finishing process as described in Penny, the Wren.

Figure 46. This Minidove was whittled out of avocado wood by Erwin Caldwell. (Photo by G. Covington.)

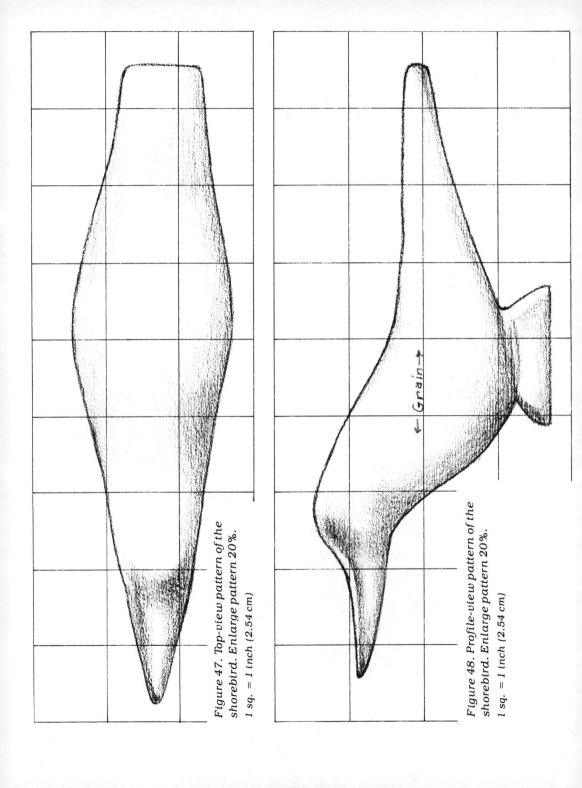

Figure 47. Top-view pattern of the shorebird. Enlarge pattern 20%.
1 sq. = 1 inch (2.54 cm)

←Grain→

Figure 48. Profile-view pattern of the shorebird. Enlarge pattern 20%.
1 sq. = 1 inch (2.54 cm)

A SHOREBIRD

This stylized version of a bird that frequents ocean and lake shores is challenging, yet not too difficult to whittle.

The one shown in Figure 49 was carved from a piece of grainy redwood. The only part of the bird that presented a problem was the long, pointed beak. Since the grain runs with the length of the wood, the narrow beak can be whittled without too much danger of breaking.

PROCEDURES FOR CARVING

Step 1. Trace and transfer both the top and profile view patterns to a block of carving wood 2¼ inches thick x 3¼ inches wide x 8½ inches (5.7 cm x 8.3 cm x 21.6 cm) long.

Step 2. Saw out the top view almost through and then saw the profile completely through.

Step 3. Round off the edges of the blocked-out shape with a knife or rasp. I used both of these tools to shape the bird shown in Figure 49.

Step 4. Use sanding sticks to finish the shaping.

FINISHING

Repeat the same process as for previous projects.

Figure 49. The finished shorebird.

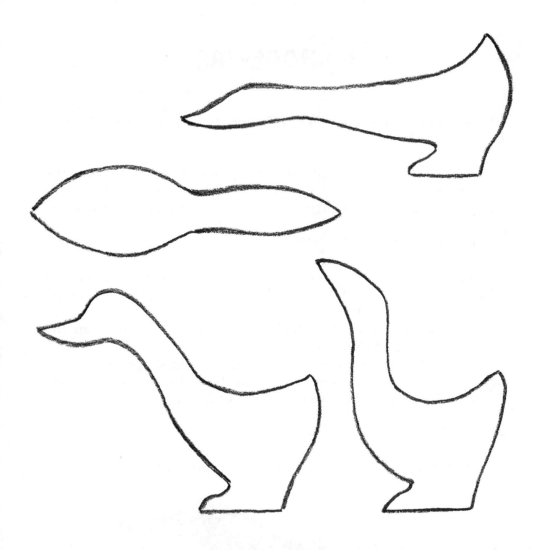

Figure 50. Full-size patterns for the little geese.

THE GOOSE AND THE GANDER

The large goose and gander are more difficult to carve than the preceding projects. Therefore, I would suggest that you start with the smaller patterns shown in Figure 50. The little goslings are much easier and faster to carve. The techniques used in whittling them will apply to the much larger birds. The finished goslings will also serve as models. Use 1-inch (2.54-cm)-thick carving wood for the little geese.

After the profile views are sawed out, much of the excess wood may be removed from the head and neck section with a coping saw. Saw about 1/16 inch (1.6 mm) outside the pattern line.

With your sharp knife, round off the body, legs, neck, and head. Random-carve from all sides until the bird is perfectly proportioned. Leave the finishing of the beak until last. The beak requires very careful carving.

FINISHING

Sand the figure until it is very smooth. Follow the same procedure as for preceding projects.

If you prefer a textured effect showing the knife cuts as pictured in Figure 51, eliminate the sandpaper. To achieve an even, smooth texture of knife cuts requires careful whittling. Slice off thin shavings to produce a finished knife-cut effect. If you are not successful with this technique, then resort to sandpaper.

Figure 51. The goose family whittled from quaking aspen.

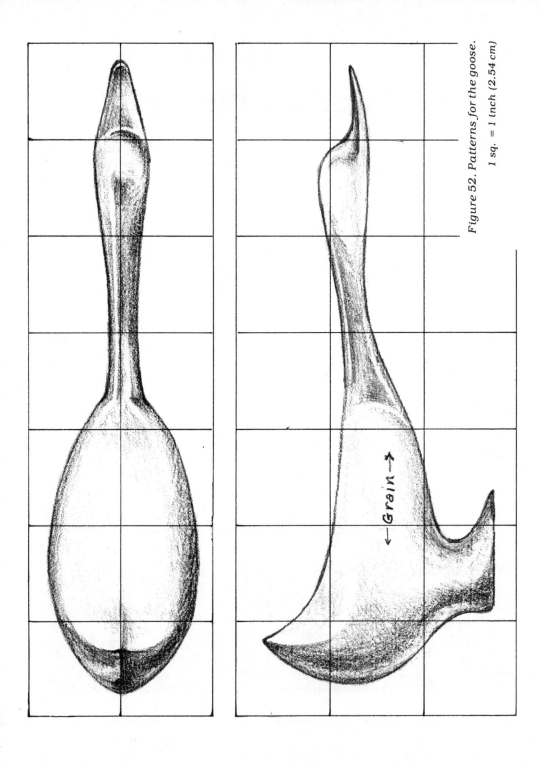

Figure 52. Patterns for the goose.
1 sq. = 1 inch (2.54 cm)

Grain →
← Grain

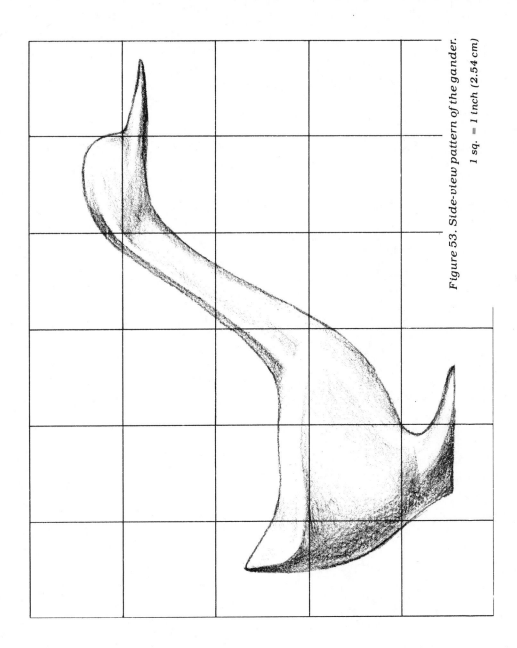

Figure 53. Side-view pattern of the gander.
1 sq. = 1 inch (2.54 cm)

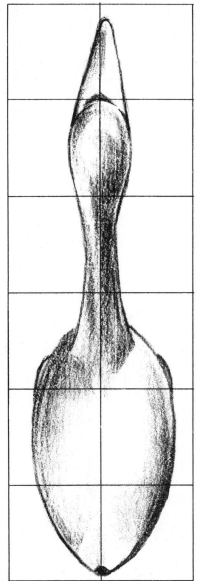

Figure 54. Top-view pattern of the gander.

1 sq. = 1 inch (2.54 cm)

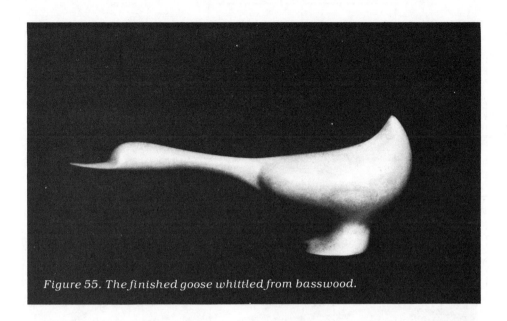

Figure 55. The finished goose whittled from basswood.

Figure 56. The finished gander carved from basswood.

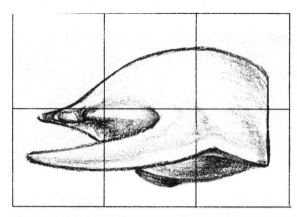

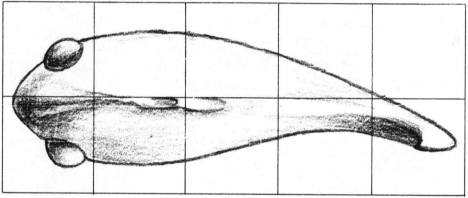

Figure 57. Top-, side-, and
rear-view patterns of Finny,
the Fish.

1 sq. = 1 inch (2.54 cm)

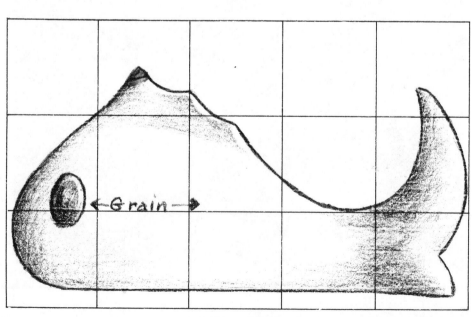

←Grain→

FINNY, THE FISH

Stylized fish are rather easy to whittle or rasp to shape. However, this finny specimen offers a distinct challenge because of its fragile tail and inlaid eyes. Be extra careful when you are carving the tail section. Since the grain runs horizontally with the length of the body, the tail is cross-grained and is easily broken.

PROCEDURES FOR CARVING

Step 1. Trace and transfer the patterns from Figure 57 to the top and side of a block of wood 1½-inches thick x 2½-inches wide x 5-inches (3.8-cm x 6.4-cm x 12.7-cm) long. I used teakwood for the fish shown in Figure 58. It has a unique grain, texture, and color.

Step 2. After sawing the top view almost through, saw out the profile view.

Step 3. Round off all edges with your knife, or rasp until the fish feels smooth and rounded in your hand.

IMPLANTING THE EYES

Step 1. To make and fit the eyes into the head requires careful workmanship. A two-tone eye implant is made as follows: Trace and transfer the eye shape from the sideview pattern, Figure 57, to a piece of light-colored wood if your fish is made from dark wood. Use contrasting pieces of wood for the eye and the pupil.

Step 2. Drill a 3/16-inch (4.8-mm)-diameter hole through the middle of the eye piece.

Step 3. Shape a short 3/16-inch (4.8-mm)-diameter dowel from a piece of dark wood. Apply a small amount of wood glue to the dowel and press it into the hole that was drilled into the middle of the eye. The two-tone eye shown in Figure 58 was made from white pine and walnut.

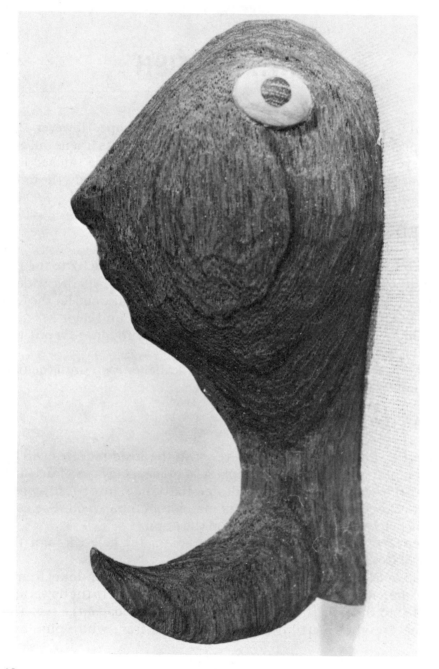

Figure 58. Finny, the Fish in natural, unfinished teakwood. (Photo by G. Covington.)

Step 4. Use the sideview pattern, Figure 57, as a template to locate the eye on the rounded fish. Trace the outline of the eye onto the head. Turn the pattern over and repeat this process on the opposite side of the head.

Step 5. Cut out shallow depressions in the fish where the eyes will be set in. This is done by making vertical incisions around the circumference of what will be the eye sockets. Next, make a series of shallow undercuts toward the middle of the eye sockets until all the cuts meet. Lift out the small piece of wood severed by the undercutting.

Step 6. Use a piece of fine sandpaper to smooth and round out the shallow eye depression.

Step 7. Sand the edges of the underside of the two-tone eye until it fits into the eye socket. Squeeze a small amount of wood glue into the socket and press fit the eye into it.

Step 8. After the glue has dried, round off the eye with a knife or small sanding stick. The finished eye should protrude about 3/16 inch (4.8-mm) above the surface of the head. The solid-colored eye, shown in Figure 59, is shaped from dark wood and fitted in the same manner as described above.

FINISHING

Sand the entire surface of the fish until it feels round and smooth. Apply successive coats of clear lacquer or varnish, sanding between coats. Rub with steel wool and wax, and then polish with a soft, clean cloth.

Figure 59. Finny whittled from natural green poplarwood by C. Bayless.

←—Grain—→

Figure 60. Patterns for the rock
dove. The grain runs with the
length of the bird. Enlarge
patterns 25%.

1 sq. = 1 inch (2.54 cm)

50

THE ROCK DOVE

Rock doves are our city pigeons. They are found in public squares and parks. They build their nests on ledges, roofs of buildings, and bridges. In the wild, they nest among the cliffs and high rocks. In Southern Utah, they appear regularly every summer to feed on the mulberries. I used a piece of white basswood for this carving. This particular piece of wood gives the bird a stark white effect. (See Figure 61.) If you have already carved the goose and gander, this dove will be rather easy for you to whittle.

PROCEDURE

Step 1. After the wood block is sawed out from compound views— top and side—whittle it to shape. Refer to Figures 60 and 61 for aid in proportioning this bird. Be very careful in shaping the beak.

Step 2. Rasp the entire bird to make it even all over.

Step 3. Sand the bird until it is satin smooth. Dampen it with a moist sponge to raise the fibres. Allow sufficient time for drying and then resand with extra-fine sandpaper.

Step 4. Spray the entire bird with clear lacquer or varnish. Apply several coats of sealer, sanding between coats.

Step 5. Apply clear paste wax and polish as described for preceding projects.

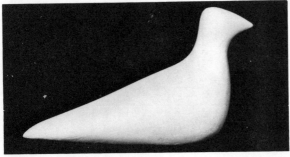

Figure 61. The finished rock dove.

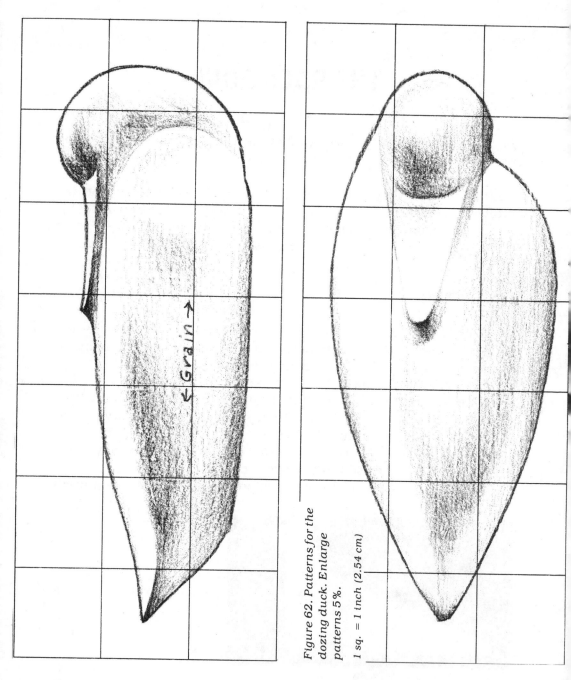

←Grain→

Figure 62. Patterns for the
dozing duck. Enlarge
patterns 5%.

1 sq. = 1 inch (2.54 cm)

THE DOZING DUCK

This stylized waterfowl is very attractive if it is fashioned from a piece of wood with a pronounced grain. (See Figure 63.) The duck shown in this figure was whittled from redwood. The delicate contour of this carved bird makes it pleasant to the eye. The graceful blend of the head and the bill flow into the body.

Select a nice piece of wood with a visible grain that is 2¼ inches thick x 2¾ inches wide x 6¼ inches (5.7 cm x 7 cm x 15.9 cm) long. Follow the same cutting-out and carving processes as described for the preceding figures.

FINISHING

Step 1. Sand until exceedingly smooth, then wipe clean with a dry cloth.

Step 2. Apply paste wax and polish to a high lustre.

Figure 63. The dozing duck whittled from redwood, waxed, and polished.

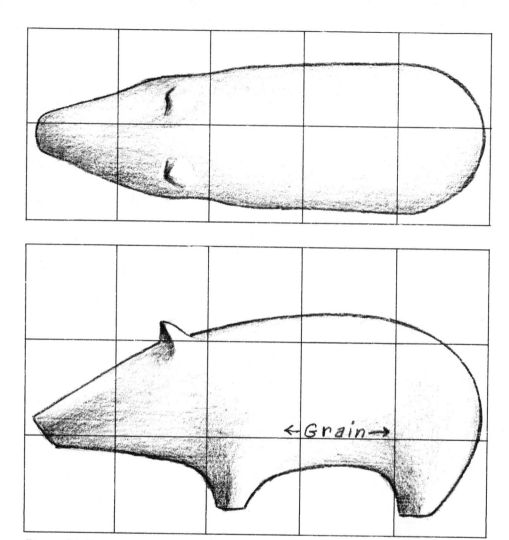

Figure 64. Patterns for Perky Pig.

1 sq. = 1 inch (2.54 cm)

PERKY PIG

We now graduate from birds to animal shapes. Perky Pig is a good beginning subject. He is simple to round into form. This abstract likeness of a pig, shaped from a piece of redwood, looks as if it were laminated.. You could experiment by gluing a variety of woods together to produce very interesting and unique effects. Perky is a pig minus a tail. This condition simplifies the carving process. Since the ears are so small, exercise great care when you are working around them.

PROCEDURES FOR CARVING

Step 1. Trace and transfer the patterns from Figure 64 to a block of carving wood that is 2 inches thick x 2½ inches wide x 5 inches (5 cm x 6.4 cm x 12.7 cm) long.

Step 2. Cut out the top view and the profile view on your bandsaw.

Step 3. Divide the rear and front legs with a coping saw. (See Figure 65.)

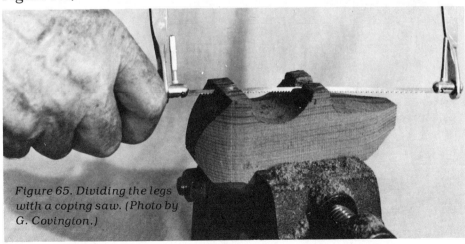

Figure 65. Dividing the legs with a coping saw. (Photo by G. Covington.)

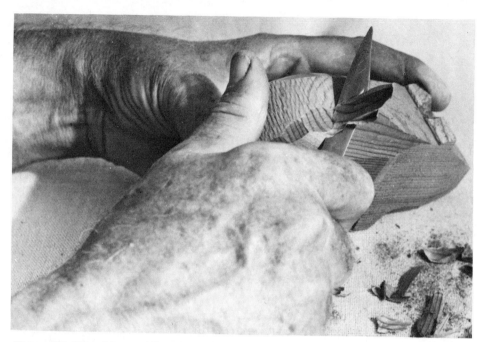

Figure 66. Roughing out the pig with a whittling knife. (Photo by G. Covington.)

Figure 67. Rounding off Perky with a coarse rasp. (Photo by G. Covington.)

56

Step 4. Round off all edges with a knife, rasp, or coarse sanding stick. (See Figures 66 and 67.)

Step 5. Use coarse and fine rasps to rub across the grain over the entire figure. (Caution: do *not* rub away the ears.) Repeat this process with medium and fine sanding sticks. The sanding-stick treatment will smooth out all the uneven places.

Step 6. Cut out between the ears with your knife. Sand the ears to shape with a fine sanding stick.

FINISHING

Step 1. Sand Perky until he is very smooth.

Step 2. Give him the wet, dry, and fine sanding treatment as explained in Penny, the Wren, Step 2, Finishing. Dust away any remaining wood particles.

Step 3. Apply several coats of clear lacquer or varnish. Sand in-between coats with very fine sandpaper and dust again.

Step 4. Rub Perky with fine steel wool impregnated with clear paste wax. Polish to a high lustre with a soft cloth.

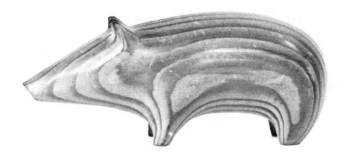

Figure 68. Perky Pig sanded and polished.

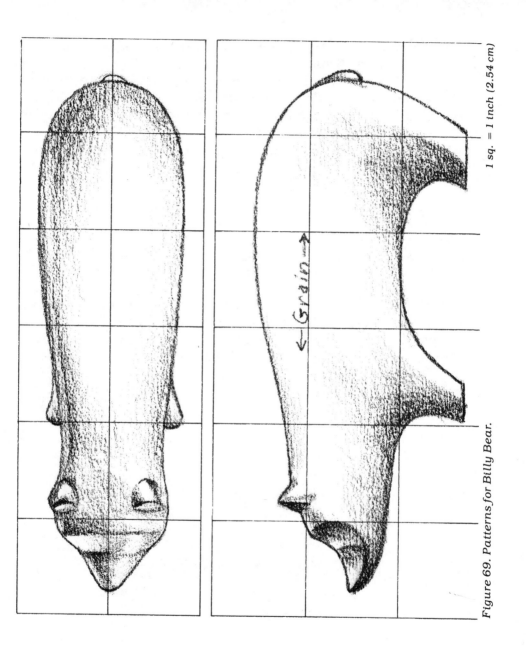

Grain

Figure 69. Patterns for Billy Bear.

BILLY BEAR

The shape of Billy Bear is very similar to that of the preceding project, Perky Pig. Add a tail to Perky and scoop out his face a little and you will have a bear. Bears and pigs are also omnivorous. They will eat most anything.

Follow the same procedure as outlined for Perky Pig for cutting out, rounding to shape, and finishing.

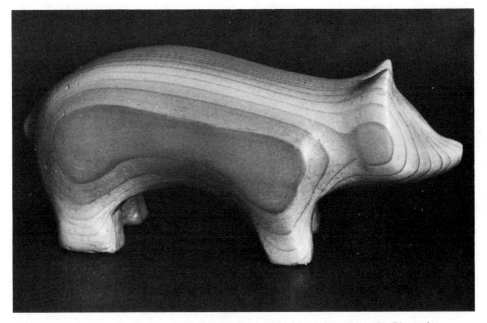

Figure 70. Billy whittled and carved from light-colored redwood. (Photo by G. Covington.)

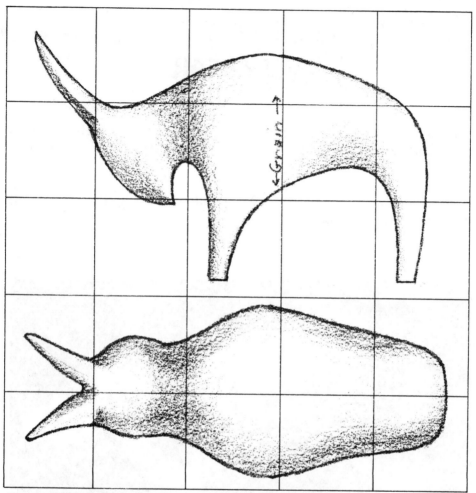

Figure 71. Patterns for Gary, the Goat.   *1 sq. = 1 inch (2.54 cm)*

GARY, THE GOAT

Except for the horns, this animal is not too difficult to whittle into shape. The horns are slightly cross-grained, which makes them rather delicate. If you carve this goat from a piece of hardwood, the danger of breaking the horns is minimized. Leave the carving of these horns for last, to avoid breakage while handling.

You will note that the hind leg is not divided into two parts. (See Figure 72.) Use a coping saw to separate the front legs. When sawing, be careful to avoid cutting into the solid hind leg.

The section between the horns is also removed with a coping saw. Saw about 1/16 inch (1.6 mm) away from the inside and outside lines drawn for the horns. You will then have plenty of stock to whittle the horns from.

Follow the same sawing out and shaping techniques as described for the preceding projects. Also finish in the same manner as explained previously.

Figure 72. Gary whittled from walnut by C. Bayless.

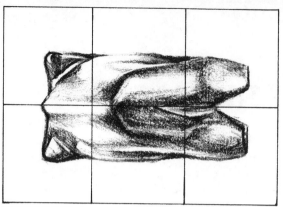

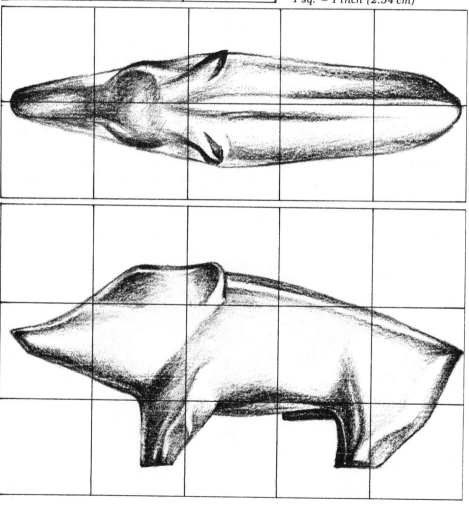

Figure 73. Patterns for Larry, the Peccary.

1 sq. = 1 inch (2.54 cm)

LARRY, THE PECCARY

The peccary, a small piglike mammal, is related to the wild pig. It is much slimmer than the domestic pig. Its long, narrow snout is designed for digging roots for food. The stylized version shown in Figure 74 was whittled from dark walnut wood.

To carve Larry, refer to the process explained earlier for Perky Pig. Also, frequently observe the patterns and the photograph of this streamlined wild pig. They will help you to visualize the finished animal.

Notice particularly the rather deep groove between the front shoulder and the head. Use your knife to cut out this groove. Also scoop out the area between the ears and the forehead with your knife.

Finish with a thorough sanding, to produce a smooth, rounded shape. Dust clean. Spray several coats of clear lacquer or varnish onto the smoothly sanded form. Rub with steel wool and wax to produce a satin finish.

Figure 74. Larry whittled out of grainy redwood. (Photo by G. Covington.)

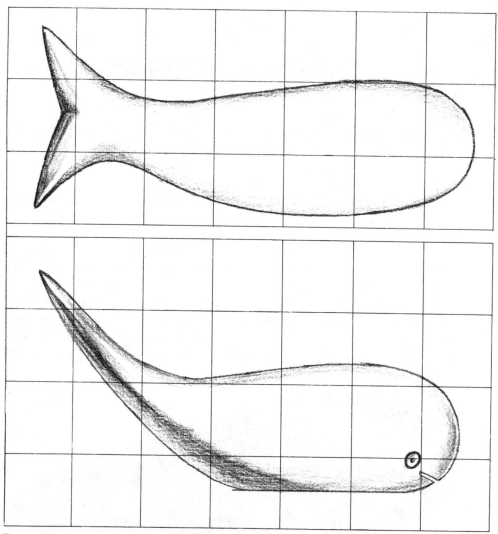

Figure 75. Patterns for Wally, the Whale. Enlarge patterns 25%.

1 sq. = 1 inch (2.54 cm)

WALLY, THE WHALE

This whale, Figure 77, was fashioned from dark walnut wood. The practice and experience you have gained from carving the preceding figures should enable you to whittle Wally with a minimum of difficulty.

After you have sawed out the top view, saw out the profile, ending with a short saw cut for the mouth. Rough out the body and tail with your knife. Leave the bottom of the whale flat.

Use rasps and sanding sticks to round and smooth Wally. Sand him until he is very smooth. Press the eyes in with a large nail set. Punch a small hole in the middle of each eye with an awl.

Follow the same finishing process as for the preceding figures.

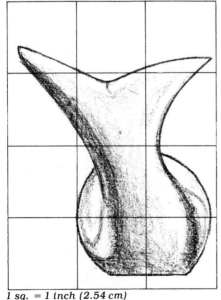

1 sq. = 1 inch (2.54 cm)

Figure 76. Tail pattern for Wally.
Enlarge pattern 25%.

Figure 77. Wally whittled by C. Bayless.

65

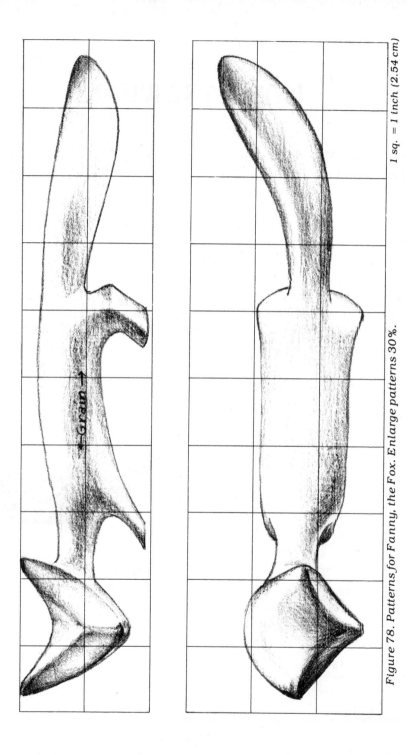

66

Figure 78. Patterns for Fanny, the Fox. Enlarge patterns 30%.

1 sq. = 1 inch (2.54 cm)

←Grain→

FANNY, THE FOX

Fanny is an eye-catcher. The ornate grain of the wood that she was carved from enhances the beauty of this stylized animal. She was whittled from redwood.

Save time and effort by sawing the fox out from two views, top and side. Her legs are not divided. This simplifies the process of shaping this unique fox.

After Fanny is completely blocked out with a band saw, whittle off all the sharp and square edges. Random carve the body, legs, tail, and head until she assumes a smooth, rounded shape, as shown in the Figure 79.

The finishing process is the same as for prior projects.

Figure 79. Fanny whittled from redwood by C. Bayless.

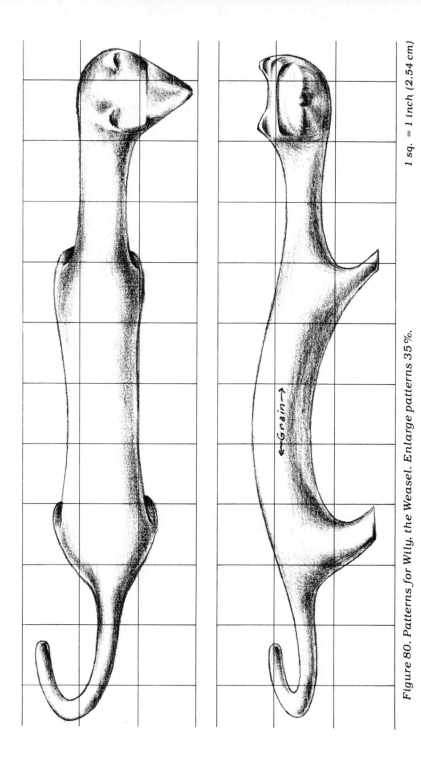

←Grain→

Figure 80. Patterns for Wily, the Weasel. Enlarge patterns 35%.

1 sq. = 1 inch (2.54 cm)

WILY, THE WEASEL

This sly little predator provides an excellent subject for an attractive carving. The weasel's brown summer fur turns white in the winter. It blends with the snow. The tip of the tail remains black. This animal's white winter coat gives us the fur that is called ermine. The highly stylized weasel shown in Figure 82 was whittled from a soft piece of redwood. It could be carved from a variety of woods. The long, slender shape also lends itself to rasp carving.

Saw out the body from two views, top and side. Unlike the previous project, Fanny, the Fox, the legs are separated with a coping saw.

Figure 81 shows Wily roughed with a rasp, ready for the finish sanding. Be very careful with the tail section. The curve of his tail is easily broken. Use a small, sharp knife or sanding sticks to finish the ears.

FINISHING

Follow the same procedure as for the preceding projects.

Figure 81. The weasel rasped to shape, ready for finishing.

Figure 82. Wily whittled out of redwood by C. Bayless.

69

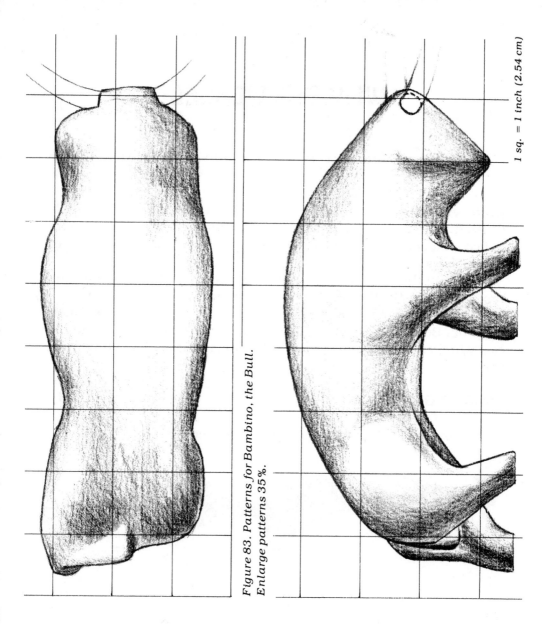

Figure 83. Patterns for Bambino, the Bull. Enlarge patterns 35%.

1 sq. = 1 inch (2.54 cm)

BAMBINO, THE BULL

This formidable-looking bovine is more difficult to carve than the preceding figures. The bull shown in Figure 85 was carved from grainy redwood. The horns were shaped from white basswood.

PROCEDURES FOR CARVING

Step 1. Trace and transfer the patterns from Figure 83 to a block of carving wood. Saw out the two views, top and side.

Step 2. Divide the legs with a coping saw. When you finish, there will be eight legs instead of four.

Step 3. Study the patterns on Figure 83 and the photo, Figure 85, then remove two legs on each side of the bull. I used a coping saw, chisel, and knife to perform this operation.

Step 4. Round Bambino to shape with knives, rasps, and sanding sticks.

Step 5. Whittle the horns out of semi-hard white wood.

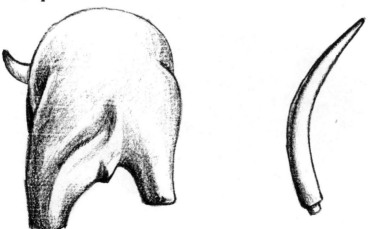

Figure 84. Rear view pattern and horn pattern. Enlarge patterns 35%.

71

FINISHING

Step 1. Sand the bull and his horns until they are very smooth, then dust away fine wood particles.

Step 2. Barely scorch the tip ends of the horns with a lighted match or a candle. Be careful not to burn too much. (See Figure 84.)

Step 3. Drill small holes on either side of the forehead to accommodate the horns. Refer to the patterns on Figure 83 for the location of these holes. Glue the horns into these holes.

Step 4. When the horns are set tight, spray the entire animal with a coat of clear lacquer or varnish. Sand the dry sealer with fine sandpaper, dust, and then apply a second coat.

Step 5. After the sealer is thoroughly dry, rub the bull with fine steel wool impregnated with paste wax.

Step 6. Polish to a high lustre with a soft clean cloth.

Figure 85. Bambino, ready for battle, carved by C. Bayless.

FREE FORMS

Whittling free-form abstracts provides good exercise in using one's imagination. Free forms do not have to conform to any preconceived patterns. The ones shown in Figure 90 were whittled out of hardwoods, walnut and bubinga.

The grain of the wood usually dictates the shape the carving assumes. Creating these abstracts presents a challenge to the carver's ability to visualize an unusual shape. The form gradually emerges from the wood as the craftsman whittles.

Unique shadow patterns can also be made from abstract forms. Refresh your memory on shadow patterns by referring to Figures 9 and 10 in the section on patterns. I applied this method of making shadow patterns to the free form on the far right in Figure 90. The result was the two unique patterns illustrated in Figures 86–86a. I carved the

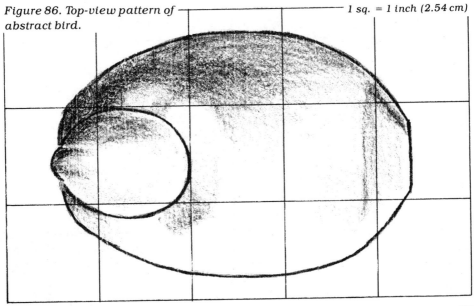

Figure 86. Top-view pattern of abstract bird.   1 sq. = 1 inch (2.54 cm)

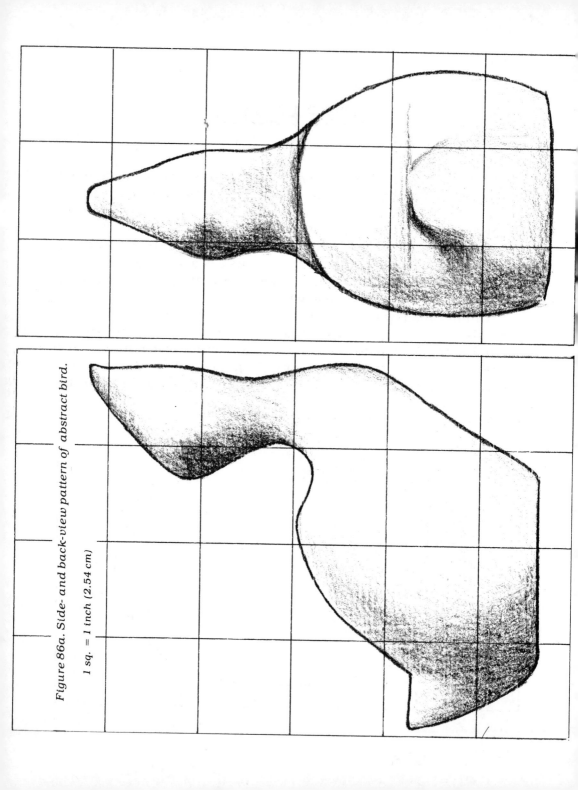

Figure 86a. Side- and back-view pattern of abstract bird.

1 sq. = 1 inch (2.54 cm)

bird, Figure 88, from a profile-view shadow, and the penguin-like form, Figure 89, from a front-view shadow.

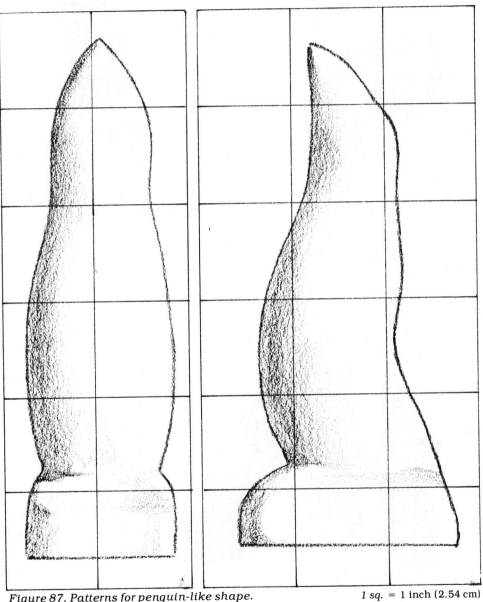

Figure 87. Patterns for penguin-like shape.

1 sq. = 1 inch (2.54 cm)

Figure 88. Abstract bird shape.

Figure 89. Abstract penguin shape.

Figure 90. Free forms whittled from hardwoods by C. Bayless.

THE TIKI

Carving a tiki is a good exercise to learn the use of the chisel and the rasp. You have already familiarized yourself with the use of the rasp, so that part will be easy. This project will also challenge you to use your imagination. Tikis can be made from tree branches, sections of old fence posts, and many other available pieces of wood.

Exaggerate the size of the nose and the lips. The more you exaggerate these features, within reason, the more attractive the tiki becomes. The size of tikis may vary from the very small to the large. I have made them so tiny that they have been worn as earrings. On the other hand, I carved a tiki that stood over five feet (1.5 m) high. Small tikis suspended from neck chains or leather thongs are worn as pendants. (See Figure 91.) A larger one can be made into a lamp as shown in Figure 92.

Following the steps shown in the photos, you will begin to carve a tiki by tracing the front view from the pattern, Figure 93.

Figure 91. Tiki necklaces stained and polished. The center figure has a small crystal rhinestone embedded between the eyes.

Figure 92. An 18-inch (35.7-cm)-high lamp base carved from a piece of two-tone redwood. I turned the mahogany base on a lathe. (Photo by G. Covington.)

Figure 93. Tiki patterns. Enlarge patterns 30%.

1 sq. = 1 inch (2.54 cm)

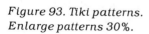

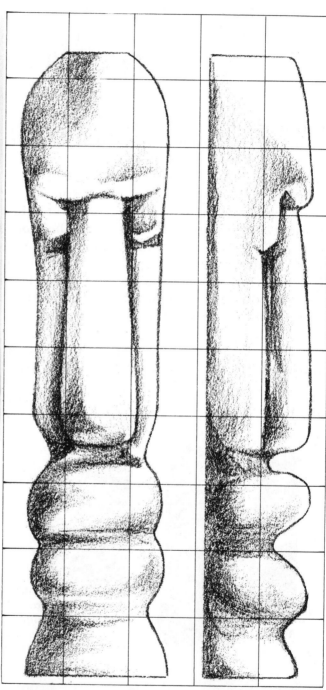

PROCEDURES FOR CARVING

Step 1. Transfer the front-view outline of the tiki to a 1¾-inch-thick (4.4-cm) piece of wood, 2½ inches wide x 9¼ inches (6.4 cm x 23.5 cm) long.

Step 2. Draw a center line down the face of the wood. This line will assist you in keeping the figure in balance as you carve.

Step 3. Refer to Figure 93 as a guide and draw the nose, eyes, and mouth lines onto the wood.

Step 4. Follow the procedure pictured in Figures 94–102. After you have completed the step-by-step carving sequence described in the above photos, you are then ready for finishing.

Figure 94. Use the rounded side of a coarse wood rasp to remove the excess wood down to the perimeter line. (Photo by G. Covington.)

Figure 95. Use a coping saw to cut the lines between the nose and upper lip. Also, make a cut through the mouth. Saw to almost one half the depth of the wood thickness.

Figure 96. Outline around the nose, eyes, and eyebrows with a straight chisel. Use the heel of your hand and do not pound too hard or you will split the wood.

80

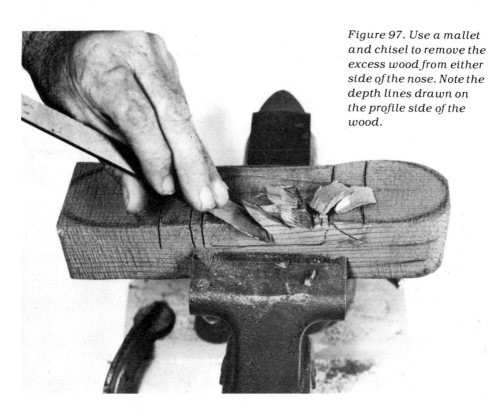

Figure 97. Use a mallet and chisel to remove the excess wood from either side of the nose. Note the depth lines drawn on the profile side of the wood.

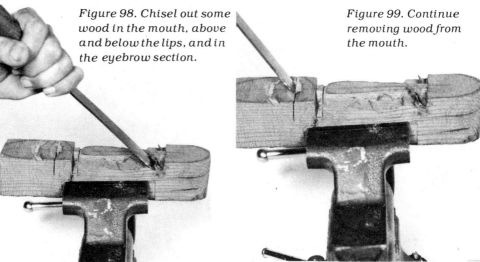

Figure 98. Chisel out some wood in the mouth, above and below the lips, and in the eyebrow section.

Figure 99. Continue removing wood from the mouth.

Figure 100. Remove more excess stock around the lips.

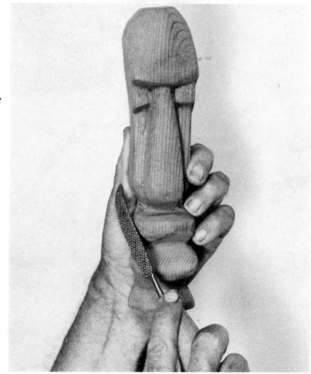

Figure 101. Rasp the carved-out figure to shape with wood rasps.

FINISHING

Tikis may be left natural, stained with wood stain, or lacquered and given a wax polish. The tiki shown in Figure 102 was left natural. The ones pictured in Figure 103 were stained dark walnut, waxed, and polished. The lamp, Figure 92, was brushed with successive coats of clear satin finish lacquer until a piano finish was achieved.

Figure 102. Tiki ready for finishing.

Figure 103. Tikis whittled out of pop-larwood, stained, and polished.

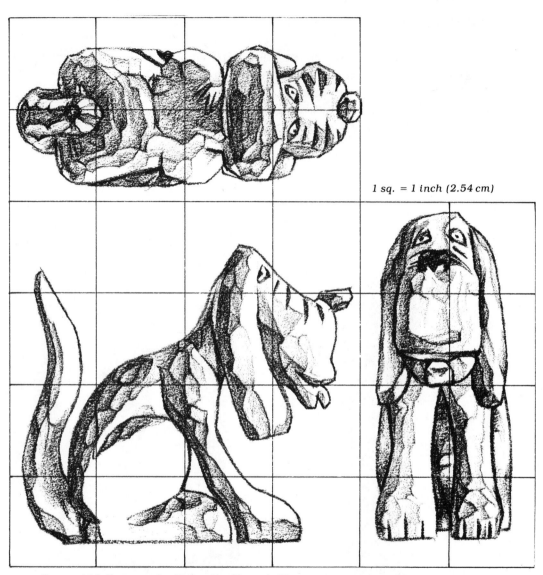

1 sq. = 1 inch (2.54 cm)

Figure 104. Patterns for Sitter, the Hound. The grain runs vertically with the tail and the legs. Enlarge patterns 5%.

SITTER, THE HOUND

Sitter, as his name implies, prefers to do just that—sit. His lolling red tongue hangs out in anticipation of receiving a choice morsel of food.

After you block out Sitter on a band saw or jigsaw, the only carving tools you will need are a coping saw and a whittling knife. Refer to the patterns shown in Figure 104. Use the coping saw to remove a narrow section from between the forelegs. (See Figure 105.)

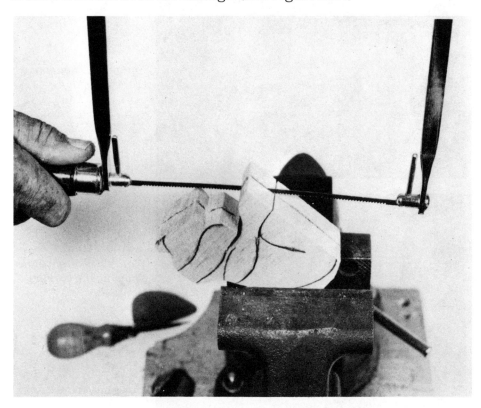

Figure 105. Sawing between the forelegs with a coping saw. Be careful not to saw into the face.

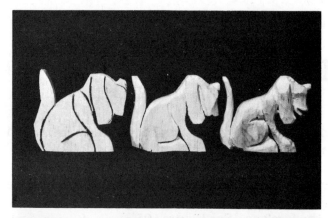

Figure 106. Profile-view of three stage carving sequence. Note the V-cuts.

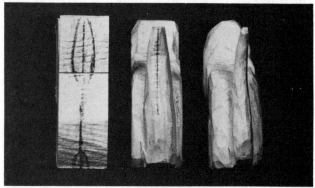

Figure 107. Rear view carved in stages.

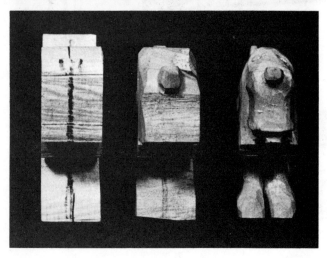

Figure 108. Front view showing the carving sequence.

Next, follow the three-stage carving sequences illustrated in Figures 106–108 inclusive. The middle model in Figure 106 shows the body and facial features outlined with V-cuts. These are made as follows: Make a shallow vertical cut on the pattern line, followed by an angle incision to meet the vertical cut at its lowest depth. It is then easy to remove the V-shaped wedge. Study the model to determine on which side of the line the vertical and angle cuts are made.

Delay the final carving of the face until last. Be careful not to cut the nose off, but if you do, glue it back into place. The break will hardly be noticeable when dry and painted.

With a pencil, mark the location of the eyes. Use a sharp pointed knife to carve small mounds around the eye dots.

FINISHING

Step 1. Carefully carve away all dirt and smudge marks with your knife.

Step 2. Spray the entire hound with a thin coat of clear lacquer or varnish to seal the wood.

Step 3. After the sealer is thoroughly dry, paint on the spots with dark brown water-base paint. Paint the tongue red and the nose black.

Step 4. With a fine-pointed brush, outline the rim of the eyes and lightly touch up the wrinkles with rather thick black paint. The paint should be rather heavy, to prevent spreading.

Step 5. Allow the spots to dry, then sand them lightly with very fine sandpaper to emphasize the highlights.

Step 6. Spray Sitter with a coat of clear lacquer or varnish.

Figure 109. Sitter, whittled from ponderosa pine. (Photo by G. Covington.)

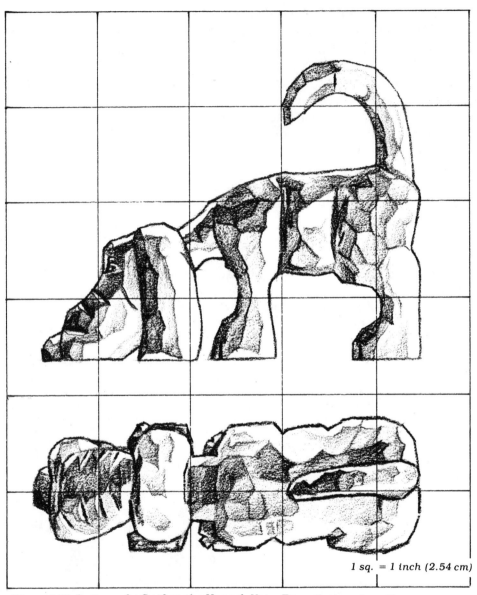

1 sq. = 1 inch (2.54 cm)

Figure 110. Patterns for Snifter, the Hound. Note: From the top view, the ears are so long that they have a slight curve upward where they meet the ground.

SNIFTER, THE HOUND

Snifter, the Hound, who always gets his man, is fun and easy to carve. I used a grainy piece of ponderosa pine for Snifter, the same wood that Sitter was carved from. This pine is not the most suitable wood for carving, but it was available in the right thickness. It also has a nice, attractive grain.

In carving the tail, care must be exercised. With the grain of the wood running crosswise at the curve, it is easy to split off the end portion. Should this happen, do not despair. Merely glue it back onto the stub. When the tail is painted, the break will not be visible.

After the silhouette is sawed out, divide the legs with a coping saw. Proceed to outline the pattern lines with V-cuts as described in Sitter, the Hound.

The whittling and finishing techniques are also the same as for Sitter, the Hound.

Figure 111. Snifter, whittled from a piece of grainy ponderosa pine. (Photo by G. Covington.)

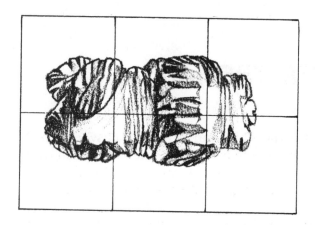

Figure 112. Patterns for Gigi, the Pekingese. The grain runs vertically with the legs and the ears.

1 sq. = 1 inch (2.54 cm)

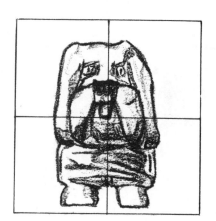

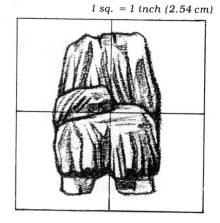

GIGI, THE PEKINGESE

At one time the Pekingese was the royal dog of China. Only individuals of royal blood were allowed to own these unusual dogs. Despite their small size, these miniature animals possess a quick temper and a pugnacious disposition.

Gigi is one of the toy breed of long-haired dogs. She has a pug face and a plume of a tail that curls over the left hip. Select a clear-grained piece of soft carving wood for Gigi. The procedure for carving her is, with several exceptions, the same as for whittling Sitter and Snifter. The exceptions are: Instead of using a coping saw to cut between this dog's legs, use your knife. Also, since Gigi's body is covered with long silky hair, simulate it with a series of irregular small V-cuts over most of her body.

FINISHING

Step 1. Mark the eyes with pencil dots. Carve away the wood around the pencil dots to form small mounds.

Step 2. Spray Gigi with a coat of clear sealer.

Step 3. Spot with dark-brown paint or stain. Refer to Figures 113 and 114 for assistance in locating the spots to paint or stain. Paint the nose black and the tongue red.

Step 4. Spray the entire figure with a coat of clear sealer.

Figure 113. Gigi from the left side, showing the position of the tail.

Figure 114. Gigi from the right side. (Photo by G. Covington.)

91

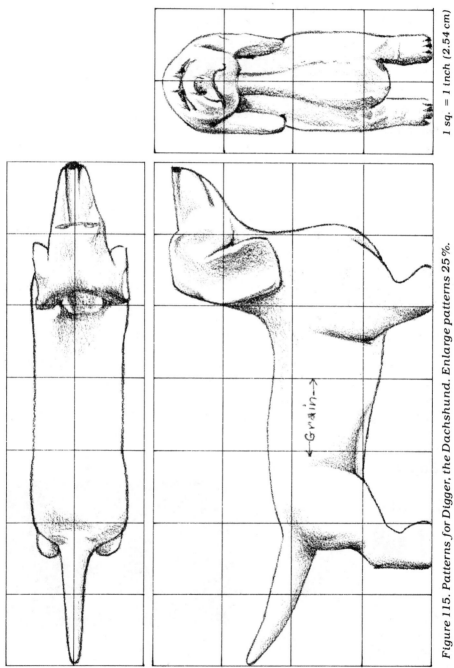

Grain→

1 sq. = 1 inch (2.54 cm)

Figure 115. Patterns for Digger, the Dachshund. Enlarge patterns 25%.

DIGGER, THE DACHSHUND

The dachshund is sometimes referred to as "a half-a-dog high and a dog-and-a-half long." It was originally bred in Europe to hunt badgers, a very fierce fighter. The dachshund's short legs enable him to pursue the badger right down the hole. In German, dachshund means "badger hound." I am partial to this stubby dog with the long ears and the pointed tail, preferring him over all of the dogs that I have carved.

I whittled Digger, shown in Figure 116, from a piece of light cream-colored basswood. The grain of the wood runs parallel with the head and the tail. There is little danger of the tail breaking. Since the legs are so short, it is easy to carve them, even though they are cross-grained.

Refer often to the patterns on Figure 115 and the photo, Figure 116, as you whittle this unique canine. In general, follow the same carving procedure as for the preceding dogs.

I gave Digger a thorough sanding and then sprayed him with two coats of clear lacquer. However, before applying the lacquer, I painted his nose black. A coat of clear paste wax further improved his appearance.

Figure 116. The finished dachshund.

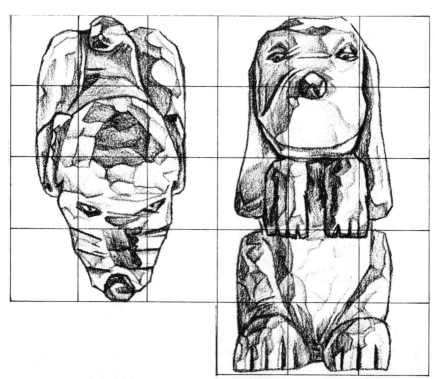

Figure 117. Top- and front-view.
patterns of Banjo, the Beggar.
Enlarge patterns 25%.

1 sq. = 1 inch (2.54 cm)

BANJO, THE BEGGAR

I started out to whittle a different kind of a dog but, somehow, I created Banjo. He emerged from a piece of 2¼-inch-thick (5.7-cm), well-seasoned white pine that had been in my shop for several years. The position of his forepaws, an afterthought, depicts him in the position of begging.

If you follow the instructions for whittling Sitter, the Hound, it should not be too difficult for you to carve a good likeness of this panhandling mutt.

Carve out the area between the legs with your whittling knife.

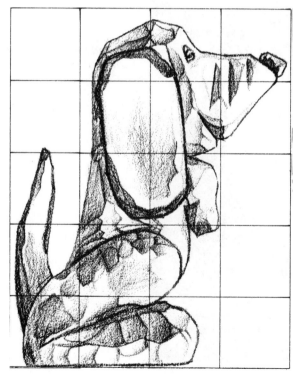

Figure 117a. Side-view pattern of Banjo, the Beggar. Enlarge pattern 25%.

1 sq. = 1 inch (2.54 cm)

FINISHING

Step 1. Carve away all dirt and smudge marks with your knife.

Step 2. Spray the entire figure with a thin coat of clear sealer.

Step 3. Paint both ears, upper half of the tail, right hip, left leg, and forepaws dark brown. Paint the nose black.

Step 4. After the paint is dry, sand the above parts to bring out the highlights. Paint the inside of the mouth red.

Step 5. Spray the entire carving with a coat of clear sealer.

Figure 118. Close-up of Banjo. (Photo by G. Covington.)

BIG CLYDE, THE CLYDESDALE

The Clydesdale, a magnificent draft horse, is admired by viewers because of its immense size, dignified bearing, and high-stepping gait. I whittled Big Clyde in caricature from a piece of sugar pine. For me, it is easier and more fun to carve in caricature style than in exact realism.

If you carefully follow the steps outlined below, you should be able to whittle Big Clyde.

PROCEDURES FOR CARVING

Step 1. After sawing out the profile, remove the excess wood from between the legs with a coping saw.

Step 2. Trace and transfer the pattern of the left hind leg from Figure 121 to the corresponding part on the sawed-out silhouette of Big Clyde.

Step 3. Use your knife to remove the rear part of the left hind leg. (See Figure 122.) Also whittle away the forepart of the right rear leg. (See Figure 123.)

Step 4. When roughing out, I like to start with the hooves and carve upward to the main body. This method makes it easier for me to proportion the horse more accurately.

The top view shown in Figure 120 will help you visualize the shape of the back. If you have a pair of outside calipers, use them to transfer the exact measurements from the patterns to the actual carving. This will help you to proportion accurately.

Step 5. After you have roughed out the legs, body, and head, sketch on the bridle and shoulder collar. Also draw the bow onto the tail. Refer to the top view, Figure 120, for the shape of the bow. Make V-cuts all around the above parts with your knife. Remove the excess wood from around these parts to make them stand out in relief. Frequently refer to the patterns and photos for assistance in visualizing the finished parts.

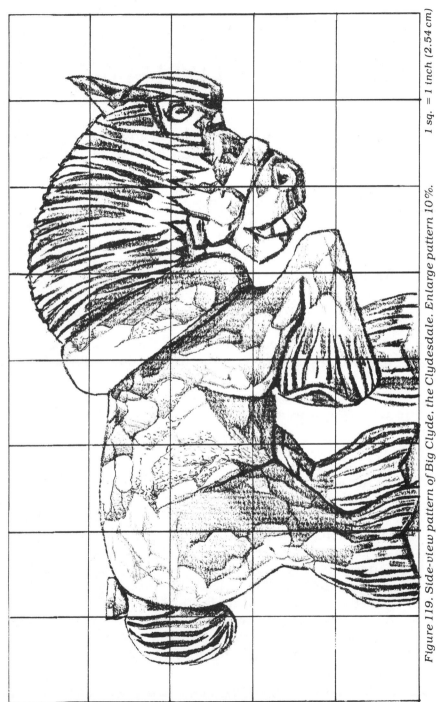

Figure 119. Side-view pattern of Big Clyde, the Clydesdale. Enlarge pattern 10%. 1 sq. = 1 inch (2.54 cm)

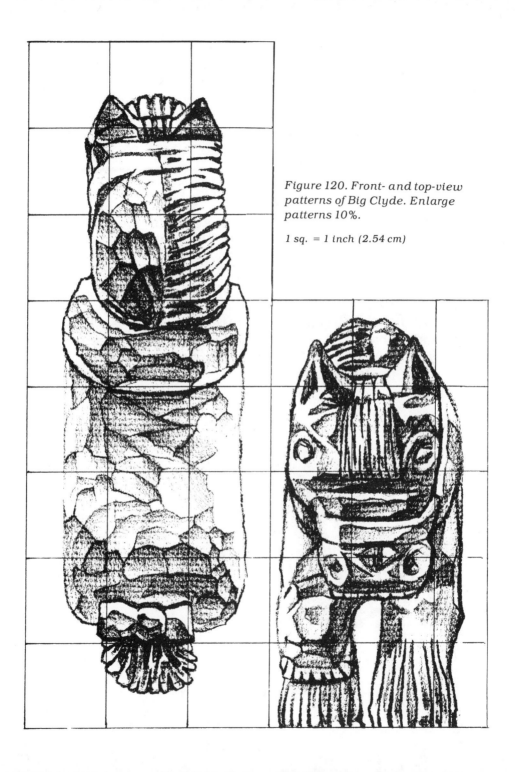

Figure 120. Front- and top-view patterns of Big Clyde. Enlarge patterns 10%.

1 sq. = 1 inch (2.54 cm)

Step 6. Continue to whittle, removing shavings at random from the hooves, legs, tail, body. and head until the animal reaches its final shape. Carefully detail bridle, collar, and bow.

Step 7. Use a pencil to mark the location of the eyes. Carve small mounds around the pencil-made dots to produce the eyeballs.

Step 8. Make a series of V-cuts to simulate hair on the mane, tail, and around and above the hooves. (Refer to Figures 119–123.)

FINISHING

Step 1. Trim off all dirt and smudge marks with your knife.

Step 2. Paint the bow and the ribbon that goes around the tail red. Use water-color or acrylic paint for these items. Also paint the middle of the bow and the eyeballs black. Color the teeth off-white.

Step 3. Allow sufficient time for the paint to dry, and then spray the horse with clear sealer.

Step 4. Paint the bridle, collar, and the exposed parts of the hooves with Vandyke-brown oil color thinned with Danish Oil or turpentine.

Step 5. Mount Big Clyde on a base of your own design.

Step 6. Spray the entire figure including the base with clear sealer.

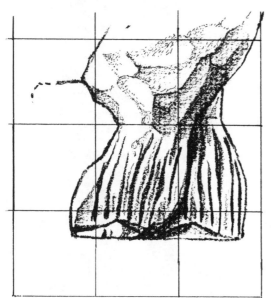

Figure 121. Left-leg pattern. Enlarge pattern 10%.

1 sq. = 1 inch (2.54 cm)

Figure 122. Left-side view of Big Clyde.

Figure 123. Right-side view.

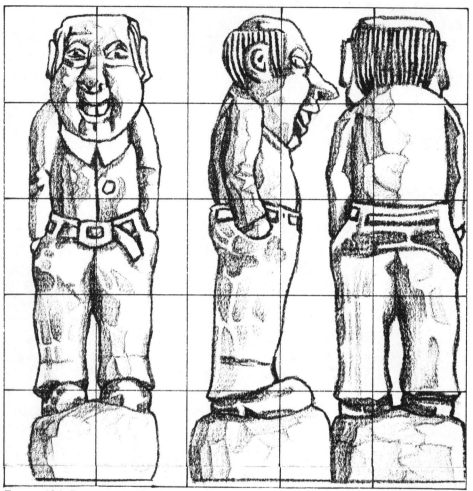

Figure 124. Patterns for Smiley.   *1 sq. = 1 inch (2.54 cm)*

SMILEY

Smiley, a toothy little fellow, serves to introduce you to the fascinating art of whittling human figures. I carved him from a piece of soft pine 1½ inches x 1½ inches x 5 inches (3.8 cm x 3.8 cm x 12.7 cm) long.

The base and the body are carved from a single piece of wood. Use your knife to remove the excess wood between the legs. Refer to the step-by-step carving sequences shown in Figures 125, 126, and 127 for aid in whittling Smiley.

Use a soft lead pencil to press in the pupils for the eyes.

Figure 125. Profile-view of three-stage carving sequence.

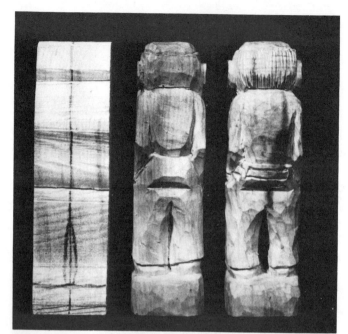

Figure 126. Rear-view carving stages.

Figure 127. Front-view carving sequence.

104

FINISHING

Step 1. Clean Smiley with your knife. Do not smooth away the knife cuts.

Step 2. Spray him with clear sealer.

Step 3. Stain or paint his hair, belt, and shoes dark brown and his trousers medium brown.

Step 4. Paint his shirt and teeth off-white and his lower lip light red. Paint the shirt button black. Leave the base natural wood color.

Step 5. Lightly sand the painted or stained areas.

Step 6. Spray the entire figure with clear sealer.

Figure 128. Smiley finished and looking happy. (Photo by G. Covington.)

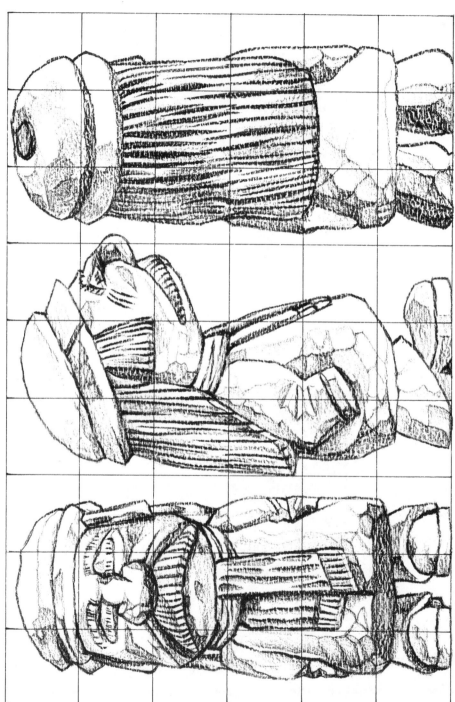

Figure 129. Patterns for Sleepy Sam. Enlarge patterns 20%.

1 sq. = 1 inch (2.54 cm)

SLEEPY SAM

Sleepy Sam, so called because he has a habit of perpetually closing his eyes. You will observe that his hair is styled after the contemporary mode. I enlarged his feet to give him good balance.

His moustache, eyebrows, and eyelids are close-together, evenly spaced V-cuts, which I made with a small knife. Also, the fringe on his scarf is a series of V-cuts. I used a ⅛-inch (3.2-mm) gouge to plough the shallow furrows in Sam's scarf.

FINISHING

Step 1. After cleaning the carving with your knife, spray Sam with a thin coat of clear sealer.

Step 2. Paint or stain his cap and scarf, except the fringe, mahogany red. Leave the fringe natural wood color.

Step 3. Carefully paint the moustache, eyebrows, and lids medium brown.

Step 4. Leave the coat and trousers natural. Paint the shoes dark brown or black.

Step 5. Lightly sand the painted or stained areas.

Step 6. Spray the finished figure with clear sealer.

Figure 130. Sleepy Sam. (Photo by G. Covington.)

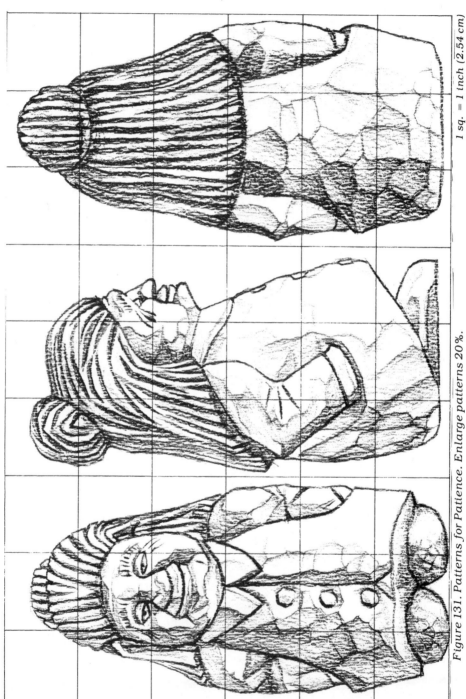

Figure 131. Patterns for Patience. Enlarge patterns 20%.

1 sq. = 1 inch (2.54 cm)

PATIENCE AND ROSEBUD

I modified the pattern for Sleepy Sam to produce Patience. Instead of a cap, I gave her a bun. Her eyes are open in contrast to Sam's. Still being in the creative mood, I decided to create a sister for Patience. (See Figure 133.) It was an easy task to convert the bun into a Spanish-style comb for Patience's sister, Rosebud. Rosebud also carries a handbag. She is also evidently wearing a man's coat because the button is on the wrong side for a woman.

After carving Sam, you should experience little difficulty whittling Patience and Rosebud. Use the patterns and the photographs, Figures 131–133, as your guides.

FINISHING

Step 1. Clean and spray the figures completely with a thin coat of clear sealer.

Step 2. Paint the hair and eyebrows medium brown. Also paint Rosebud's handbag dark brown and her comb black.

Step 3. Stain the shoes mahogany red and the coat buttons black. Leave the coat's natural wood color.

Step 4. Lightly sand the painted and stained parts.

Step 5. Spray the carvings competely with clear sealer.

Figure 132. Patience.
(Photo by G. Covington.)

Figure 133. Rosebud.
(Photo by G. Covington.)

110

COUSIN HARRY

This is another hands-in-the-pockets carving. Hiding the hands simplifies the whittling of Cousin Harry. Also, covering much of the face with a moustache and a beard makes it easier to carve the face.

A short section of a tree branch served as stock for Harry's hat, which I whittled separately from his head. After carving the hat, I flattened the underside of it and the crown of the head on a disc sander. This was done to insure a tight fit between these two surfaces. Then I drilled a ¼-inch (6.4-mm)-diameter hole ⅜ inch (9.5 mm) deep into the underside of the hat and into the crown of the head. These holes will later serve to hold a short dowel.

I used a series of irregular V-cuts to simulate hair, eyebrows and beard.

FINISHING

Step 1. Spray the hat with flat black enamel. If you do not have this item, coat the hat with black, water based paint.

Step 2. Seal the head and body.

Step 3. Paint or stain the hair, eyebrows, moustache, belt, and shoes dark brown.

Step 4. Paint or stain the coat and trousers light tan. Leave the shirt natural. Paint the shirt button black.

Step 5. Lightly rub all the painted or stained parts with fine sandpaper. Be certain to include the hat.

Step 6. Apply a thin coat of sealer to all parts except the hat.

Step 7. Dowel and glue the hat to the head. If you have a long enough vise, press the hat onto the head. Insert a piece of heavy paper or leather between the crown of the hat and the jaw of the vise. This will protect the hat from damage. Leave Cousin Harry in the vise until the glue is dry. Should you lack a large vise, use your hand to press the hat to the head. Hold in place until the glue sets.

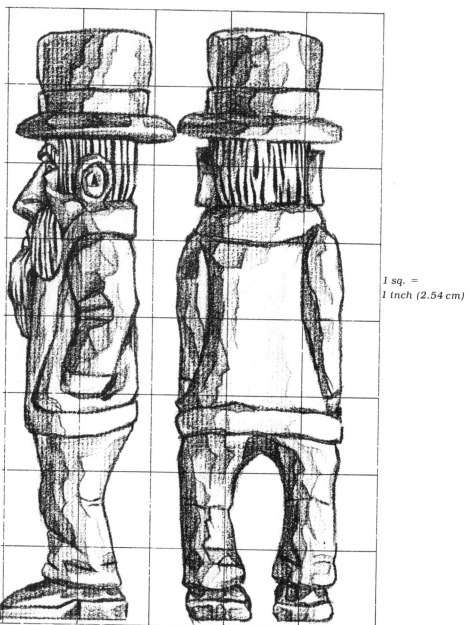

1 sq. =
1 inch (2.54 cm)

*Figure 134. Side- and back-view patterns of Cousin Harry.
Enlarge patterns 20%.*

Figure 134a. Front-view pattern of Cousin Harry. Enlarge pattern 20%.

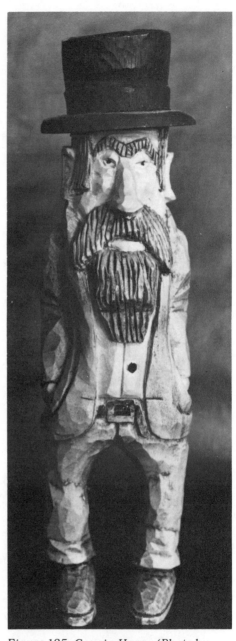

Figure 135. Cousin Harry. (Photo by G. Covington.)

113

Figure 136. Chief Toquer. (Photo by G. Covington.)

CHIEF TOQUER

Chief Toquer was the name of an Indian who was leader of a tribe in Southern Utah. Toquerville, a unique community near Zion National Park, derives its name from this colorful Indian chief.

Frequently refer to the patterns and the photo—Figures 136, 136a, and 137—and follow the same carving plan described for preceding figures. The hat is also carved separately and then glued and dowelled to the head. (See Cousin Harry.)

FINISHING

Step 1. Clean and seal the carving.

Step 2. Paint or stain the jacket and trousers medium brown. Color the hair and boots dark brown, the hat black, and the braid ties bright red.

Step 3. After a light sanding of the painted or stained parts, spray the figure with a thin coat of clear sealer.

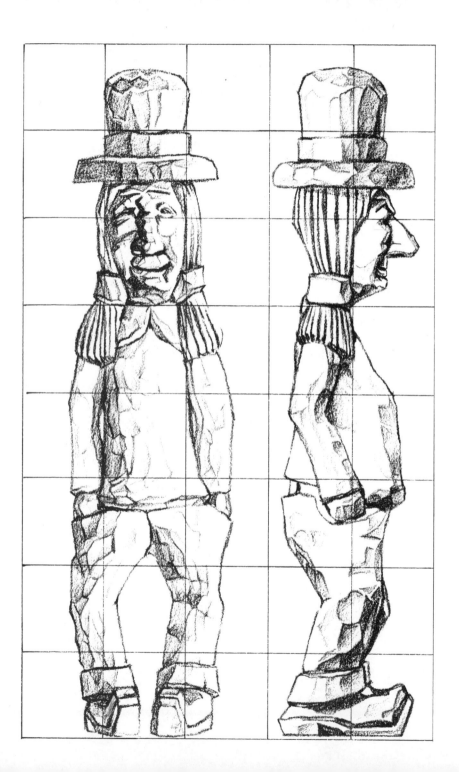

Figure 137 and 137a. Patterns for Chief Toquer. Enlarge patterns 10%

1 sq. = 1 inch (2.54 cm)

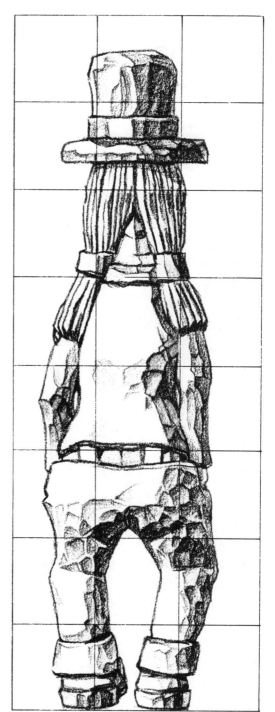

Figure 138. Patterns for Princess Toquerina. Enlarge patterns 15%.

1 sq. = 1 inch (2.54 cm)

118

PRINCESS TOQUERINA

This happy Indian maid is interesting to carve. Her long colorful braids dress her up nicely.

Texture the ends of her braids with a series of evenly spaced V-cuts. The right hand, extending over the braid, requires extra care in carving, so finish it last.

Use a ¼-inch (6.4-mm)-wide gouge to make the folds in the skirt. First anchor the figure securely in a vise. Then start at the lower edge

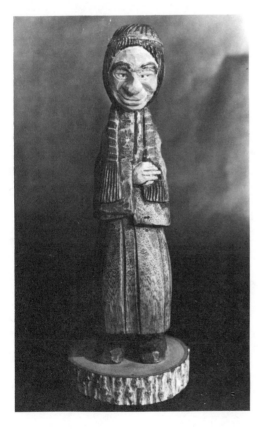

Figure 139. Princess Toquerina whittled out of avocado wood. The break in her little finger was caused by a boring beetle. (Photo by G. Covington.)

of her skirt and plough shallow furrows upward toward the waist. (See Figure 138.) Outline these folds with narrow V-grooves made with a small V-gouge or a sharp detail knife.

FINISHING

Step 1. Clean and seal the figure.

Step 2. Stain or paint the waist and skirt medium brown. Color the hair and boots black.

Step 3. Paint the braid wrappings, alternating red and green.

Step 4. Lightly sand the hair, body, and shoes to bring out the highlights.

Step 5. Spray the entire figure with a thin coat of clear sealer.

COWPOKE CHARLEY

Cowboy figures appeal to most everyone. These Western characters represent rugged individualists. Cowboys are by far my most popular creations. The body and face of the cowboy lend themselves to rather gross exaggeration. Charley's bowed legs give the impression that he has spent most of his life in the saddle.

If you have already whittled the other human figures that are shown in this book, Charley's body should not prove to be too difficult for you to carve. Since the head is more difficult, I will give step-by-step instructions for it.

I suggest that you start with the half-size patterns, Figure 140, then carve from a full-size profile. (See pages 13–15.) The neck hole for the half-size is approximately ⅜ of an inch (9.5-mm) in diameter. In a full-size profile it measures ⅝ of an inch (16 mm) in diameter.

The head can be carved as part of the body or separately. I prefer the latter method. If the head is ruined during your first attempt, no great loss, merely whittle another. The experience gained more than compensates for any loss in time.

After you have carved the body, follow the step-by-step instructions given below for carving the head.

PROCEDURES FOR CARVING

Step 1. Trace and transfer the profile-view pattern of the head to a straight-grained piece of carving wood. Basswood is preferred. The grain of the wood should run vertically from the neck to the crown of the hat.

Step 2. Saw out the silhouette of the head. Draw a center line to position the nose and the neck.

Step 3. Remove the excess wood on either side of the neck with a coping saw or knife.

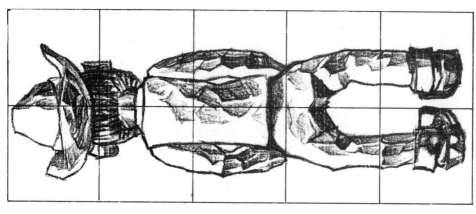

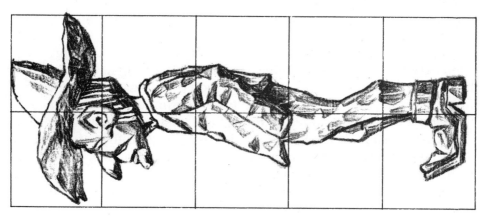

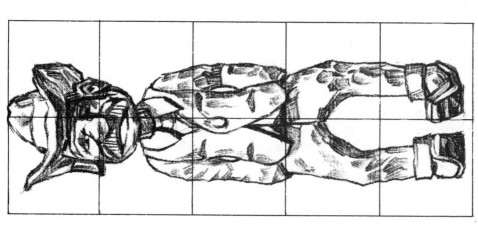

1 sq. = 2 inches (5.08 cm)

Figure 140. Half-size patterns of Cowpoke Charley. Enlarge patterns 50%.

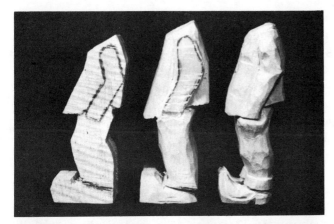

Figure 141. Profile view of three-stage carving sequence.

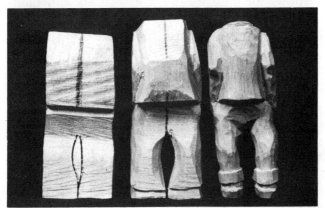

Figure 142. Rear view of Charley, showing carving stages.

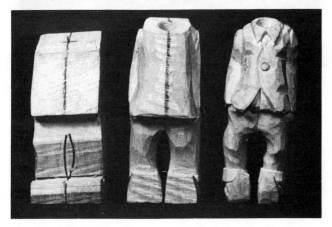

Figure 143. Front view of carving sequence.

Step 4. Carve wood away to form the crown of the hat. Scoop out the brim with a small gouge. (See Figure 145, right-hand head.)

Step 5. From the side-view pattern (Figure 140) trace and transfer the outline of the ear onto either side of the face. Rough out the area around the ears with your knife. (See center head, Figure 144.)

Step 6. Outline the nose with a pencil. (Refer to Figure 146.) Remove the excess wood from either side of the nose.

Step 7. Random carve until the face looks like the one in the center in Figure 146.

Step 8. Complete the carving of the face, commencing with the nose as the focal point and eventually ending with the ears. Refer frequently to the patterns and photos accompanying this project. The close-ups of the heads shown in Figures 147 and 148 are especially helpful.

Step 9. Carve in the hair, eyebrows, and moustache with small V-cuts.

Step 10. Mark the locations of the pupils of the eyes with a soft pencil. Deepen the pupils by pressing them in with a sharp awl.

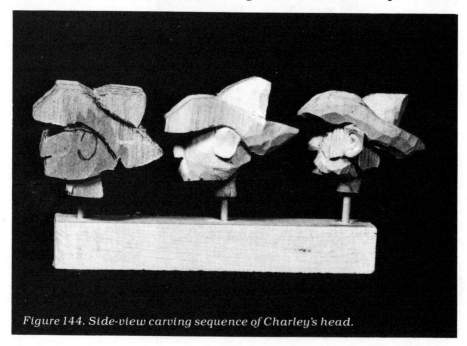

Figure 144. Side-view carving sequence of Charley's head.

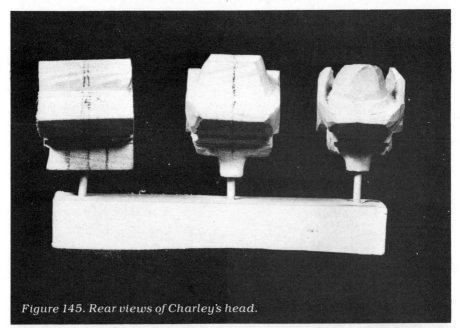

Figure 145. Rear views of Charley's head.

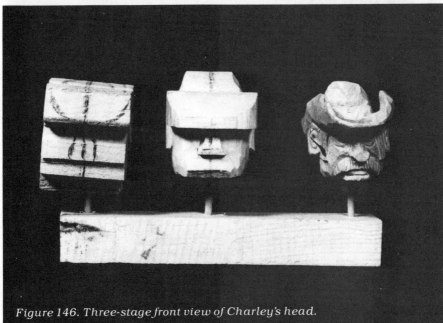

Figure 146. Three-stage front view of Charley's head.

Figure 147. Close-up of Charley's face. Note the deep knife cuts which serve to accentuate the facial features.

Figure 148. Profile view of the upper part of Charley's body and his head. A well-carved face should reveal from a side view most of the prominent facial features.

FINISHING

Step 1. During the final stages of the carving make certain your fingers are clean so no smudge marks will be transferred from them to the wood. Carefully trim the figure to emphasize the fact that it is a whittled project by making distinct knife cuts.

Step 2. When Charley is carved to your satisfaction, spray him with a thin coat of clear lacquer or varnish.

Step 3. Stain or paint the boots, vest, and hat Vandyke brown. Color the trousers, hair, eyebrow, and moustache medium brown. Leave the shirt natural wood color or paint it off-white. Paint the tie red and the vest button black.

Step 4. When the stain or paint is thoroughly dry, rub it lightly with fine sandpaper to bring out the highlights and to emphasize the knife cuts. (See Figure 149.)

Step 5. If you wish, mount Charley on a base of your own design. Leave the base natural wood color.

Figure 149. The finished carving of Cowpoke Charley. He is mounted onto a base for better balance.

Figure 150. Two variations on Charley.

127

INDEX